Sigmund Freud

In this clear and concise volume, Susan Sugarman introduces the work of Sigmund Freud and keenly illustrates the impact his pioneering contributions have had on the way we think about ourselves and each other.

Part of the Routledge Introductions to Contemporary Psychoanalysis series, this book sees Sugarman offer a comprehensive overview of Freud's major theories, their clinical application, and their empirical reach. She highlights the ways in which his work is commonly misinterpreted and expertly guides the reader through his key publications on not only his general theory but also neuroses, dreams, ordinary waking mental life, and civilization and society. Considering Freud's body of work as a whole, she explores the observations and reasoning that led him to the questions he raised and the conclusions he reached, showing the rich and nuanced approach in his writing.

Sigmund Freud: A Contemporary Introduction is an essential read for psychoanalysts, both in practice and in training, as well as students and scholars looking to understand the legacy of Freud's work.

Susan Sugarman is Professor of Psychology at Princeton University, USA, and a former Fulbright and Guggenheim fellow. She is known for her close studies of Freud's theory.

Routledge Introductions to Contemporary Psychoanalysis

Aner Govrin, Ph.D. Series Editor
Yael Peri Herzovich, Ph.D. Executive Editor
Itamar Ezer Assistant Editor

"Routledge Introductions to Contemporary Psychoanalysis" is one of the prominent psychoanalytic publishing ventures of our day. It will comprise dozens of books that will serve as concise introductions dedicated to influential concepts, theories, leading figures, and techniques in psychoanalysis covering every important aspect of psychoanalysis.

The length of each book is fixed at 40,000 words.

The series' books are designed to be easily accessible to provide informative answers in various areas of psychoanalytic thought. Each book will provide updated ideas on topics relevant to contemporary psychoanalysis – from the unconscious and dreams, projective identification and eating disorders, through neuropsychoanalysis, colonialism, and spiritual-sensitive psychoanalysis. Books will also be dedicated to prominent figures in the field, such as Melanie Klein, Jaque Lacan, Sandor Ferenczi, Otto Kernberg, and Michael Eigen.

Not serving solely as an introduction for beginners, the purpose of the series is to offer compendiums of information on particular topics within different psychoanalytic schools. We ask authors to review a topic but also address the readers with their own personal views and contribution to the specific chosen field. Books will make intricate ideas comprehensible without compromising their complexity.

We aim to make contemporary psychoanalysis more accessible to both clinicians and the general educated public.

Aner Govrin – Editor

Jungian Psychoanalysis: A Contemporary Introduction
Mark Winborn

Sigmund Freud: A Contemporary Introduction
Susan Sugarman

Sigmund Freud

A Contemporary Introduction

Susan Sugarman

LONDON AND NEW YORK

Designed cover image: Cover image © Michal Heiman, *Asylum 1855–2020, The Sleeper* (video, psychoanalytic sofa and Plate 34), exhibition view, Herzliya Museum of Contemporary Art, 2017

First published 2024
by Routledge
4 Park Square, Milton Park, Abingdon, Oxon OX14 4RN

and by Routledge
605 Third Avenue, New York, NY 10158

Routledge is an imprint of the Taylor & Francis Group, an informa business

British Library Cataloguing-in-Publication Data
Names: Sugarman, Susan, author.
Title: Sigmund Freud : a contemporary introduction / Susan Sugarman.
Description: 1 Edition. | New York, NY : Routledge, 2024. | Series: Routledge introductions to contemporary psychoanalysis | Includes bibliographical references and index.
Identifiers: LCCN 2023014247 (print) | LCCN 2023014248 (ebook) | ISBN 9781032495569 (hardback) | ISBN 9781032495477 (paperback) | ISBN 9781003394402 (ebook)
Subjects: LCSH: Freud, Sigmund, 1856-1939. | Psychoanalysis—History.
Classification: LCC BF109.F74 S84 2024 (print) | LCC BF109.F74 (ebook) | DDC 150.19/52092—dc23/eng/20230608
LC record available at https://lccn.loc.gov/2023014247
LC ebook record available at https://lccn.loc.gov/2023014248

ISBN: 978-1-032-49556-9 (hbk)
ISBN: 978-1-032-49547-7 (pbk)
ISBN: 978-1-003-39440-2 (ebk)

DOI: 10.4324/9781003394402

Typeset in Times New Roman
by Apex CoVantage, LLC

Contents

Introduction   1

PART I
Freud's Theory of the Mind   5

1   The Pleasure Principle   7

2   Instincts as Stimuli to the Mind   19

3   The Interests That Vie Within Our Minds:
Id, Ego, and Superego   25

4   Revisions and Consolidation of the Theory   33

PART II
Empirical Inquiries   41

5   Freud on Neuroses: The Case of Fräulein
Elisabeth von R.   43

6   Freud on Dreams   57

7   Freud on Ordinary Waking Mental Life   73

8   Freud on Civilization and Society   89

    Essential Freud   101

    References   *107*
    Index   *111*

Introduction

Who are we? The question is timeless. Psychological answers, framed from the vantage point of how the mind works, date at least to Aristotle and appear in other ancient philosophies such as Stoicism and Epicureanism. They are embedded in the writings of great Western thinkers up through the ages, including Descartes, Hobbes, Locke, Spinoza, Hume, Rousseau, Kant, Mill, and Nietzsche. Sigmund Freud (1956–1939) embodies that grand-theoretic tradition, asking who we are essentially, scrutinizing his assumptions for their worth and coherence, and trying to build from those rudiments to the complexity we know as human mental life.

The tradition appears to stop with him as well. Although psychoanalysis, while branching into different schools, continued to produce theorists, they mainly elaborated or presented alternatives to components of Freud's vision. They did not intend grand theory, and many, as we will see in Part I here, failed to recognize what Freud accomplished with his.

Freud, however, offers a grand theory of humans that departed from its predecessors. His theory, a system of interconnected concepts, is wholly psychological, unlike those of his grand-theoretic predecessors, who were philosophers. It explains behavior and experience, all behavior and experience. There are no interstitial categorizations, no attempts to deploy predefined aspects of mental life like thought, perception, or passion. All there is is behavior and explanation in terms of

DOI: 10.4324/9781003394402-1

what the mind did and how and why it did it, to produce the behavior.

Indicative of the difference is his treatment of the building blocks of our mental life whose designation he shares with his predecessors. Like some of them, he gives priority in our mental makeup to our experience of pleasure and pain. According to his forebears, our thought and action would have no motive without passion, passion, in turn, anchored in our experience of pleasure and pain. He aligns with some also in recognizing the same biologically determined instincts operating within us and impacting the mind. For Aristotle, those were reproduction and the need for food; for Kant, sexual love and a love for life. For Freud, they will be the impulsions toward sex, or more broadly union, and individual survival, or what he came to call the ego instincts.

Only Freud, however, turned such elements into a body of ideas that helps explain our mental life. For example, only he makes the point that the existence of inborn instinctual urges – toward food or sex, for example – in a creature with a mind, pushes that mind to develop. The attempt to think psychologically, and as a way of explaining human doings, was new.

Psychoanalysis has by now developed well past Freud. Myriad schools and directions of practice exist within it. At the same time, it is anchored in Freud. It wouldn't have existed without him. It is worth understanding Freud, from the ground up, not to set the clock back, but to revitalize the present.

§

That is the task of this book, to immerse readers in the stuff of Freud's thought and work, building from where he started to the theoretical edifice and empirical contribution he left us. Chapters are organized around iconic texts of Freud's, with the intention of showing not only the results at which he arrives, but the way he gets there.

Part I presents a chronological reconstruction of his general theory of the mind. It observes his progressive addition of layers to the theory, beginning with his "pleasure principle" (Chapter 1), then turning to the impetus he calls instinct (Chapter 2) and the different interests we try to satisfy as we act in the world, which he came to call id, ego, and superego (Chapter 3). Chapter 4 presents his later revisions of the theory and a consolidation of it as it appeared at the end of his career.

Part II considers a sampling of Freud's empirical endeavors, demonstrating both the dynamic interplay among theory, practice, and observation in his work and the ever-widening scope of his concerns. Chapter 5 examines one of his case histories, allowing readers to appreciate him as a clinician and to grapple with the breeding ground of his more general thought. Chapter 6 engages his first more general foray, his investigation of dreams. Chapter 7 explores some of his investigations of ordinary waking mental life, including parapraxes – momentary mental glitches like slips of the tongue – and our capacity for humor, as well as how we get lost in a book. Chapter 8 considers his sweeping *Civilization and its discontents*, in which he brings his accumulated psychological inquiries to bear on the current state and future of society.

The book concludes with a distillation of what remains essential in Freud.

Part I

Freud's Theory of the Mind

Chapter 1

The Pleasure Principle

In the scorching summer of 1880, a young Viennese woman known in the psychoanalytic literature as Anna O. suffered an excruciating inability to drink, despite tormenting thirst. She had no organic abnormality. "She would take up the glass of water she longed for, but as soon as it touched her lips, she would push it away," wrote her physician Josef Breuer (Breuer and Freud, 1895, p. 34), soon to become Sigmund Freud's mentor. She suffered a disorder known since antiquity as hysteria, a nervous illness manifesting in psychosomatic symptoms.

Anna, in addition to enduring debilitating symptoms, fell prey to states of absence of which she had no recollection after normal consciousness returned. During one of them a year later, and in Breuer's presence, she talked of a former lady companion she disliked whose despicable dog she had once found drinking from a glass. Recalling the episode now, with the full force of the venomous disgust she had withheld at the time out of politeness, she awoke pleading for water, never to avoid it again. After that first serendipitous success, Breuer purposefully prompted Anna to explore, under spontaneous or induced hypnosis, the events her symptoms called to mind.

Until Breuer's, and later Freud's, efforts, the medical establishment largely dismissed hysterias as meaningless mental detritus associated with previous emotional shock. It ascribed the wildly maladaptive effects to degeneracy of the nervous

DOI: 10.4324/9781003394402-3

system. Breuer and Freud (1895) showed both characterizations to be wrong.

Hysterical symptoms arise, they contended, as internally coherent, yet outwardly dysfunctional, overreactions to memories prompted by the suppression of powerful emotion at the time of the triggering events. As Freud would understand the process later, the mind would push – *repress* – the painful memory from awareness, sometimes replacing it, in the case of hysteria and other neuroses, with a different pain. It was emotionally easier for Anna O. to contend with a crippling aversion to drinking than it was for her to negotiate the rage and terror extending to and beyond the lady companion.

The claim of neural degeneracy, meanwhile, was obviated by the normal and even elevated intellectual function exhibited by some patients outside their symptoms. For example, Anna O. exhibited heightened fluency in English, a foreign language to her, while beset by her symptoms. In paradoxical juxtapositions like that, Freud saw grounds for a specifically psychological explanation of the disease. Because patients, when hypnotized, could recover memories that otherwise eluded them, he reasoned, some force must have been keeping the memories from conscious awareness. He imagined the force to represent a *resistance* to the content. The resistance was driven by interests – like Anna O.'s concern for her propriety and safety that appeared to restrain her in the episode with the lady companion's dog – that would lead people to perceive the content as threatening (Freud, 1909a, Lecture II).

The case of Anna O. and others that followed cemented Freud's revolutionary and iconic belief that a large portion of human mental life occurs outside awareness. It occurs *unconsciously* and can influence our conscious lives.

The ideas of unconscious functioning and of repression and resistance have become part of the standard lexicon of not only any form of depth psychotherapy, including psychoanalysis, but also common parlance. We say things like, "I must have repressed that," and refer to unconscious motives and the like. Freud, as he developed psychoanalysis, as both an intellectual discipline and psychotherapeutic method, changed the way we think.

There is a tendency among those either coming to Freud for the first time or presenting him to such an audience to see his conceptual offering as a catalogue of terms like the preceding ones. To those we might add others, such as his "pleasure principle" and the triumvirate of id, ego, and superego. The list goes on. Freud had a long career, spanning over 40 years in psychoanalysis alone. He devised many terms for ease of exposition. But despite the way he is sometimes presented, the terms exist on the periphery of his thought, as only expository conveniences.

His general theory is an organic whole, an elegant system with interacting parts. Moreover, it grew as he wrote, treated more patients, and investigated additional behaviors and experiences of both the healthy and ill. It grew in concentric circles. Although he sometimes revised the way he saw things, mostly he added nuance and integration to what he had already constructed. To understand Freud's theory, then, and to understand his work, which is anchored in the theory – his clinical contributions and his other investigations – is to decipher that evolving system.

The system is built around first principles: regularities our thought and behavior observe that can't be broken down into further parts and figure in all we do. When an assertion is a first principle, other propositions follow from it or connect to it. In this and the following three chapters, we accompany Freud as he constructs his theory and repeatedly questions which principles of human mental life truly capture who we are and are sufficiently basic to span our lives and extend to all our behavior.

His first fully psychological conception, originally presented at the end of *The Interpretation of Dreams* (1900), achieves its most compact expression in his 1911 paper, "Formulations on two principles in mental functioning." We will track the primary section of that paper in attempting to decipher the *pleasure principle*, the earliest principle he articulated.[1]

"Psychical activity draws back from any event which might arouse unpleasure," he says (1911, p. 219) in articulating the organizing principle that remained, throughout all his subsequent renderings of the theory, the most basic one in our psychology. The flip side of the principle is that we try to cultivate pleasure. However, that is a more elusive and also less urgent goal.[2] Important in the dual definition is that Freud's pleasure principle refers above all to our virtually reflexive tendency to stave off pain. It does not, contrary to some highly reductive popular conceptions we will consider later, refer to the pursuit of pleasure for its own sake.

Why the Pleasure Principle Is Basic

Why would Freud have determined the pleasure principle to be the most basic stratum of our psychological makeup? He offers several considerations.

First, mental illness involves escaping from reality and replacing it with something more palatable. Neurotic people, for example, turn from reality, in whole or in part, because they cannot bear it. Even when, in their symptoms, they replace it with a still disagreeable alternative, they are replacing it with something they find better in some way, as Anna O. did her revulsion to drinking. Compulsive hand-washers who live in terror of infection achieve two benefits from their debilitating syndrome. They both mask a deeper seated fear and, by washing, ward off the fear they are conscious of – the threat of infection – when they cannot perceive their real fear. The victory is temporary, because, as long as the real problem remains, the superficial fear will rise again.

Additionally, in ordinary day-to-day life, we naturally avoid the unpleasant. We avoid distasteful tasks and distressing thoughts. We try to avoid or at least mitigate unappealing situations and cultivate the ones we like. Children, more vividly than adults, avoid what they disdain and strive for what they enjoy. Even when we take risks or undermine ourselves in other ways, we typically do so in the interest of a different gain. A skydiver loves the thrill of it. Or we might become self-denying or self-destructive through a desire to alleviate guilt or to act out frustration we cannot direct elsewhere.

More elementally, the pleasure principle, in this early formulation of Freud's, expresses the most basic function of the nervous system, to discharge stimuli. The dynamic can be seen in the operation of the reflex. Stimuli impinge on the body's receptors, where they create a state of physical tension. Reflexes, like blinking in response to light, unpremeditatedly discharge the excitation. Freud, on that model, initially coupled pleasure with the lowering of excitation. Although he later elaborated that rudimentary conception (see Chapter 4 here), he continued to accord priority in mental life to the discharge of excitation.

Development Toward a Reality Principle

Were we equipped only to discharge excitation or immediately turn from the unpleasant in any other way, we would soon fail to attain relief. The mind must complicate to negotiate that situation. Freud tells a hypothetical story about how the change occurs.

He takes as a (hypothetical) starting point a mind that observes only the function of discharging stimuli. It is a mind, in other words, functioning strictly according to the pleasure principle and equipped with only the simplest machinery a mind can have, the reflex.

As long as reflexive action is sufficient to lower the irritation produced by stimuli, all goes well: tension is reduced, pleasure is attained. When your hand strikes a hot stove, you jerk it back; the pain is gone or at least lowered. But in a complex organism like a human baby, stimuli emanate from inside, as well as from without. When they come from the inside, as hunger does for example, no simple action can banish them. You cannot withdraw from a hunger pang. Freud calls such endogenously generated, inescapable stimuli *needs*. Because babies' actions are initially limited to little beyond the reflex, they cannot satisfy the need. The environment steps in to provide the wanted satisfaction. The baby, however, knows nothing of the arrangement. It just experiences satisfaction where it once felt pain.

Nonetheless, Freud continues in his hypothetical story, any need, like hunger, having once been fulfilled, automatically evokes a memory of its fulfillment the next time the need arises. The experience of the combination – of the need and the remembered image of its satisfaction – results in an impulse to reexperience the satisfied state. A hunger pang will be accompanied by an evocation of satiety. Freud labels that impulse, to reexperience the desired state, the first embodiment of the *wish*.

Initially, Freud says, again imagining the hypothetically most primitive state, we not only feel impelled toward the remembered image of satisfaction. We reproduce the entire perceptual experience of it. We hallucinate it. Once we re-experience the need – for satiety, say – we immediately evoke the need's fulfillment, just as a reflex immediately discharges an external stimulus that has triggered it.

Although the idea of hallucination may conjure for readers a complicated and elusive process, Freud sees in it the simplest of mechanisms. At least in theory, it offers the shortest path to the fulfillment of a need, namely an instantaneous one. It conforms entirely to the pleasure principle, in the ideal accordance with which we would admit no pain at all. Instantaneous hallucination of satiety upon the onset of hunger would prevent us from feeling its pain.

In part, Freud wants us only to imagine the simplest way in which an entity could operate, because from there he can tell us what has to go into an organism that would do more. On the other hand, he presents evidence that something close to such a primitive state might actually exist. Hallucination dominates dreams, which, as strictly unconscious and involuntary, disclose our most primitive mental characteristics.

Hallucination, of course, cannot relieve actual needs, Freud says resuming his developmental story. Were babies, when hungry, only to hallucinate satiety, they would eventually feel pain they could not ignore. Even though a highly attentive environment might anticipate their needs and supply the necessary satisfaction much of the time, no caregiver is perfect, and all relax the symbiotic bond in time.

Therefore, babies need to come to discern when a satisfaction they perceive, for instance a hallucinated one, is not real. To do that, they must let in pain rather than shut it out. Rather than enjoy the pleasure a hallucinated satisfaction may bring, for instance of satiety, they must let themselves feel the pang – the hunger – the absence of real satisfaction produces. Recognizing the satisfaction's absence, they can then apply themselves to bring it about. Thus is the *reality principle* born. We look not only for pleasure, but for pleasure that is real.

Freud admits that no organism ever in fact observes only the pleasure principle; it would meet a quick end were it to do so. Babies with a capacity only to hallucinate their way out of hunger would starve. He is describing a theoretical point of origin, which, however, is approximated by babies in arms whose needs are readily attended to (1911, Note 4, pp. 219–220).

Sequelae of the Reality Principle

In Freud's hypothetical story, the accession to the reality principle initiates many further transformations. His presentation of one, the birth of cognitive capability, provides an opportunity to clarify the import of his assertion of the pleasure principle's dominance.

The most direct result of our recognizing the need to assure our satisfactions, he says, would be our effort to change the real circumstances when we find satisfaction wanting. With that step we transition from being the passive recipient of our experience to being the engineer of it. To take that step, we need the mental accoutrements that will allow us to effect the changes we want.

We would have needed[3] sense organs directed toward the outer world, along with *consciousness*, to register the qualities of the environment thus detected. We would also have required the ability to search the environment for the qualities we needed for the task at hand, for instance appeasing our hunger; the function in question is *attention*. We would have developed a system of notation – *memory* – to keep track of the results of our searches and eventually *judgment* to decide the worth of our ideas.

Additionally, reflexive motor discharge, for example flailing or crying when we are in pain, would have given way eventually to *action* for purposes remembered in advance, so that we might re-find in reality the satisfaction we once achieved there. Thus, for example, babies' reflexive crying when hungry would segue to crying intentionally so as to bring the providers of relief (Freud, 1911, p. 221). *Thought*, Freud adds, would have evolved to support the development of action. It would have allowed us to envision the results of our actions in advance, as well as serving to restrain impulsive action while we worked things out.

Significant in that dense and astonishing list is Freud's insistence on relegating all the cognitive capabilities we think define us and to which we owe our survival – who could escape prey without a sensory system? – to a secondary position in our psychological makeup. By contrast, a whole line of thinking in modern psychoanalysis, called ego psychology, claims exactly the opposite. It prioritizes the capabilities that allow us to navigate our surroundings. We are, according to Heinz Hartmann (1939), born with latent perception, language, thinking, and other cognitive capacities that facilitate our engagement with the outside world. Should that world prove hospitable, those pregiven capabilities then unfold as a matter of course, not, as he believes Freud would have it, as part of a circuitous route to the satisfaction of frustrated needs.

Freud, however, would not dispute that our cognitive capabilities may be partly built in by this point in evolution and that they likely flower in a nurturing surround (e.g., Freud, 1940, p. 185). He is addressing something else, namely the *psychological* priority of the pleasure principle in our mental ecology. Pleasure and pain, he says, are more primordial psychologically than are specific sensory qualities. Their primacy is reflected in the original purpose of the nervous system to discharge stimuli, the result bringing relief, or pleasure. It is likewise reflected in the withdrawal of sufferers of neurosis and psychosis from reality in favor of a more agreeable fantasy.

We can perhaps best appreciate that psychological primacy if we compare its consequences with those of the opposite alignment of priorities.

If, as Freud believes, the processing of pleasure and pain is more primordial psychologically than is the processing of specific sensory qualities, then, hypothetically, the simplest conceivable psychological organization would have only that function. It would only discharge the stimuli that impinged on it, for example, reflexively withdrawing the impinged upon receptor: jerking back an arm, blinking an eye. To carry out that function, an organism would not need to know the source of, or anything else about, the stimuli. It would just discharge what disturbed it. The organism wouldn't last very long, because it would have no means of distinguishing helpful from harmful stimuli. Lacking that discrimination, it would be unable to prevent itself from destruction. Therefore, only those organisms exist that have some reality function and the equipment for carrying it out.

Now imagine the opposite arrangement of capabilities: an organism that had external sensation and even the capacity for action, but no urge toward discharge. In other words, it did not observe a pleasure principle. That scenario has no coherence. The reason is that, in the absence of an urge toward discharge – toward change – it would have no incentive to detect anything or to act. Freud's pleasure principle provides the incentive, and he reasonably conceives it as the more basic psychological function.[4]

Writers like Hartmann, who see in Freud's depiction of our infancy as driven by the pleasure principle an overemphasis on need states, make a second mistake. In misreading him to say babies are driven exhaustively by their biological needs, they ignore his critical point. Those needs are vital in forcing us to build a mind. Hunger unsatisfied will eventually force us to build capacities to address it, according to Freud's hypothetical formulation.

There is a broader way in which Freud's pleasure principle gets misinterpreted. In specifying that we are ubiquitously driven by the avoidance of pain (or, when possible, the procurement of pleasure), Freud is misunderstood to say we are driven *only* by the quest for pleasure. In the light of that reading, psychoanalytic theorists after Freud made a point of showing how we enter the world wired for purposes other than the satisfaction of simple pleasures.

For instance, we are wired, according to those theorists, for social interaction. René Spitz (1965) emphasizes that babies naturally incline toward establishing a connection with others, a position later echoed by theorists of attachment (e.g., Bowlby, 1969) and later investigators of the mother-infant relationship (e.g., Stern, 1985). Ronald Fairbairn (1994, p. 131ff) emphasizes that, although pleasure might be one form through which we connect with others, we will retain connections by other means if we must. Thus, for instance, abused children willingly repeat painful experiences if doing so will preserve their bond with their significant other; they do that rather than seek an alternative love object who might supply pleasure rather than pain.

All those authors have contributed important insights into our early relationships with others and precipitated advances in the therapy designed around the insights. But they err in imagining their observations or therapeutic innovations undercut the primacy of the pleasure principle as Freud understood it.

Freud was no stranger to the idea that people might actively seek experiences that would seem to others to bring only pain. People with neuroses, like Anna O., may succumb to painful and debilitating symptoms. They do so, analysis reveals, because they cannot face a more frightening dread. That is to say that pain or discomfort is being endured to some further end: the blocking of a more intractable fear in the case of neurotic symptoms. For a behavior to meet a purpose is for it to accomplish something that is wanted. To accomplish, or even only to strive toward, what is wanted is, in turn, to obviate pain or pursue pleasure – it is to act in accordance with the pleasure principle. That framework easily accommodates Fairbairn's observation that children may cling to abusive caregivers. They are gaining, or trying to gain, something else out of the clinging, however ill chosen.

Notes

1 A forerunner to the pleasure principle appears still earlier in Freud's (1895) unpublished "Project for a scientific psychology," whose physiological underpinnings he subsequently disavowed.

2 See Freud's (1930) *Civilization and Its Discontents*, Chapter II, for further elaboration on the asymmetrical sides of the pleasure principle, also touched on here in Chapter 4.

3 Freud leaves ambiguous whether he is discussing a hypothetical individual development or a hypothetical evolution of the species. I am reverting to species evolution at this juncture in the narrative, as Freud seems to do. The difference is not important. It is hypothetical either way, and the psychological portrayal he wants to impart is clear.

4 Melanie Klein (e.g., 1957), in her vision of babies' original universe – the "good breast" vs. the "bad breast," or simply the good vs. the bad – evokes Freud's pleasure principle. Her vision aligns with the idea that initially we want to "eat it" or "spit it out," a later rendering of Freud's (1925, p. 237) of the earliest manifestations of the pleasure principle: we either like it or we dislike it, and if we dislike it, we want to be rid of it. That determination takes priority, for both Klein and Freud, over ego functions like the detections Hartmann wants to endow us with.

Chapter 2

Instincts as Stimuli to the Mind[1]

If our mind observes a pleasure principle – if it always strives in some respect to avoid unpleasure or cultivate pleasure – then something must spur the principle to action. That impetus can come from two directions, as the previous discussion suggests: from without, like a beam of light, or from within, like a hunger pang. Those sources differ with respect to what is needed to discharge them. We can withdraw from external stimuli, which makes them comparatively easy to discharge, whereas we cannot withdraw from an internal stimulus. We can blink to eliminate the irritation caused by a light beam. Hunger must be satisfied. Freud called the impulse triggered by the latter variety of stimulus *instinct* (*Trieb* in the original German).[2]

In a usage he recognizes as idiosyncratic, "instinct" refers to the mind's registration of stimuli flowing from an organ of the body, resulting in a demand for work aimed toward the relief of the demand (Freud, 1915, p. 122). Hunger and thirst are examples, as is the full panoply of sexual impulses, including the stirrings of attraction, babies' lust for thumb-sucking and physical contact, and the canonical sexual act. Each of those impulsions is driven by an urge from within. Although stimuli emanating from the external world – sights, sounds, smells, and things touched – also impinge on the mind, they do not as a rule produce the demand for work fomented by the needs arising from interior stimuli.

DOI: 10.4324/9781003394402-4

The latter – instincts – therefore impel the development of the mind, contrary to the conventional view that new input from the external world motivates change (Freud, 1915, p. 120). As we saw in connection with the reality principle, individuals, to satisfy their basic needs, must renounce the primordial function of warding off stimuli in favor of determining the real circumstances and trying to alter them. To satisfy hunger in the long-term, we must allow in its pain, discern the absence of real nourishment, and set about obtaining the real thing.

Basal Instincts

Instincts come from different sources and have different aims and objects, though all have the overarching aim of satisfaction. Hunger, for instance, is generated by a process in the stomach. The instinct to quell it aims at achieving satiety – eliminating the hunger – which it can do through the object we know as food. Given that infinitely many impulsions may arise from within, including, for example, an impulsion to play, to seek social contact, and so on, then we could in theory distinguish infinitely many discrete instincts. There could be a play instinct, a social instinct, a humorous instinct, and so on.

Freud wondered whether all the possibilities might not trace to just a few basic types. Those types, in turn, would define the major axes along which our lives run. He identifies two such types in his early theory, the sexual and ego, or self-preservative, instincts.

He cites as the main justification for that division the conflicts he has regularly observed in his patients between interests aligned with the two categories. Patients in treatment uncover long-buried lusts and animosities toward their prominent others, while also uncovering dread of those feelings. The dread arises from their perception of the feelings as inappropriate or at risk for serious repercussions. In Freud's taxonomy, the lusts and animosities, as part of our relations with others, express

the sexual instinct. The fear of those feelings and their consequences, a self-protective impulse, manifests the ego instinct.
The prospect that the two categories of instinct can conflict suggests they form discrete categories.

The division also echoes the conventional distinction
between hunger and love, where hunger connotes the ego
instinct and love connotes the sexual instincts. Additionally, the
separation follows biologically. Biology distinguishes between
those functions that advance the interests of the individual and
those directed toward the preservation of the species. The ego
instincts aim toward the sustenance of the individual, while the
sexual instincts help perpetuate the species.

Both classes of instincts function from birth, and each under-
goes a lengthy and somewhat separate development. The ascen-
sion of the reality principle, discussed in the previous chapter,
is an example of development of the ego instincts, though it
also serves the sexual instincts with its assurance that perceived
sexual objects are real, rather than fantasied. The sexual instinct
develops from largely autoerotic satisfactions – pleasure gained
from stimulation to different parts of the body – to the pursuit of
external objects recognized as such, like caregivers and friends,
and ultimately relationships, including the mature sexual act, with
objects outside the family. In between those two phases, *narcissism*, or the recognition of and investment in the self, develops
(Freud, 1914). Though it is normally eclipsed by our love of others, it remains to some extent with all of us through life.

Freud's notion of sexuality is broad. It includes both physical manifestations, like stimulation to especially sensitive, or
erotogenic, zones, which extend well beyond the genitalia, and
the full range of emotional relations of which we are capable.
Freud (1940, p. 153) notes, in the latter connection, the rival-
ries for affection that can arise among even very small children
in the nursery, as well as the Oedipal drama through which he
describes our complicated relationship with our parents (e.g.,
Freud, 1909a, Lecture IV, 1923).

What Freud Intends by Basal Instincts

Freud's delineation of the sexual and ego instincts as the basal ones has resulted in another ubiquitous misreading of his intent: that everything we do, think, or feel reduces to an impetus toward sex or survival.[3] Far from so reducing us, he was attempting to identify building blocks of the mind so elemental they trace all the way back to our animal ancestors. He stipulated that the nervous system seeks first and foremost to discharge the tensions that arise within it (see the preceding chapter). What Freud terms "instincts" produce impelling tensions from within. Those stimuli, by contrast with external stimuli, do not easily find discharge and therefore place demands on the mind. Wanting next to know which kinds of instincts exist that reduce to no simpler constituents, he makes a strong case for the primacy of sexual and self-preservative, or ego, instincts.

When he delineates those as basal, he means that one or the other, or both, run through every impulsion we have, no matter how ostensibly far removed it is from the idea of sex or (self-) survival. Even scientific curiosity (Freud, 1909a, Lecture V) and the sensitivity to beauty (Freud, 1905a, p. 156 n2 and p. 209) might derive historically from the realm of sexual feeling, Freud imagines.

Those and related claims have incurred extensive disapprobation from commentators. For example, some later psychoanalytic writers disagree that drives[4] form the core of our emotional life (e.g., Bion, 1962; Erikson, 1950; Klein, 1957; Kohut, 1984) and protest what they see as Freud's reduction of the higher and finer in mental life to those drives. We are more absorbed by our relations with others than we are with drives (e.g., Bowlby, 1969; Mahler, 1968), they think, or our drives are more likely the result of our experiences, rather than the other way around (e.g., Hartmann, 1939; Jacobson, 1964). We aspire to and achieve great things; art and science cannot be reduced to instinctual appetites (e.g., Hartmann, 1939; Loewald, 1988).

Those who disparage Freud's emphasis on instincts over adaptive capabilities like babies' cognitive apparatus or their connection with love objects set up false dichotomies. In propounding instincts, Freud is attempting to specify the architecture of the system. He is not saying what is important in life. Instincts make the system go. Their manifestations develop throughout life. When one path to fulfillment is blocked, we form another, resulting in myriad elaborations of the original impetus.

Consistent with those considerations, Freud, in ascribing our intellectual and cultural achievements to the sublimation – rechanneling – of our root instincts, was not reducing those achievements to the instincts. In postulating the continuities he did, he pointed out the very richness critics would deny his account. His argument is that if all our strivings ultimately derive from sexual or self-preservative (ego) instincts, then we ought to be able to identify traces of either or both impulsions in all human striving.

That sense of Freud's analysis is well demonstrated by his passing commentary on beauty (Freud, 1905a, p. 156 n2 and p. 209; 1930, Chapter II). Beauty, he says, has a mildly intoxicating quality whose origin is obscure. Imagine, for instance, the mild narcosis we may feel when beholding a spectacular sunset. He wonders whether our capacity to be thus moved by beauty – whether the stirrings we feel – might not trace to the field of sexual feeling. Historically, he speculates, beauty might have evolved as a property attaching to secondary sexual characteristics, such as the face or the figure, features designed to attract, as opposed to those evolved to serve the sexual act itself. Freud, although easily misread, again reductively, to have claimed there is something sexual about what we find beautiful (e.g., Beigel, 1953), is among the few who have raised, let alone grappled with, the questions of what the sensibility consists of and where is might have come from.

Notes

1 This chapter tracks Freud's (1915) "Instincts and their vicissitudes."
2 Although some contemporary authors prefer to translate *Trieb* as "drive" rather than "instinct," I follow the usage of James Strachey, Freud's

premier translator and the chief editor and translator of *The Standard Edition of the Complete Psychological Works of Sigmund Freud* (1981). The term "instinct" captures the sense of a boundary concept between the psychological and biological intended by Freud (1915). "Drive," according to some of the authors who use it, conveys the unmediated quality of the impulse that Freud also intends and avoids the suggestion they detect in the English "instinct" of the narrower fixed action pattern in animals common in contemporary biological usages (e.g., Lear, 2000; Mitchell and Black, 1995).

3   After Freud began later to write about aggression (see Chapter 4, p. 29, and Chapter 8 of this book), he was again misread reductively to be saying we are dominated by aggressive, as well as sexual, impulses.

4   "instincts" in the usage I am following here; see note 2, this chapter. I follow commentators' usage when I am discussing them.

Chapter 3

The Interests That Vie Within Our Minds

Id, Ego, and Superego[1]

The most basic motor of our action, according to Freud, is the pleasure principle: our attempt to avoid pain and, secondarily, to cultivate pleasure. That striving is instigated by stimuli, the most enduring of which are what he calls instincts, urges from within that can't be resolved easily and are destined always to reappear. He distinguishes as the most elemental categories of instincts the sexual and self-preservative, or ego, instincts.

We develop past those rudiments through various mechanisms, among them our acknowledgment of painful stimuli, which gradually precipitates the acquisitions of the reality principle in Freud's hypothetical telling. Our attempts to negotiate instinctual stimuli, like hunger, are a subcategory of that dynamic.

The mind that eventually develops is multi-faceted and multi-layered. Freud eventually came to characterize it with respect to three different aims and methods of operation he called id, ego, and superego (Freud, 1923). He devised the taxonomy to be able to characterize the mental dynamics he saw exposed by his treatment of the psychoneuroses.

Originally, he distinguished only between what was conscious and what was unconscious. Anna O., for example, was conscious of her inability to drink, but the presumptive reason for the inhibition – her disgust at her lady companion's dog's

DOI: 10.4324/9781003394402-5

drinking from a glass – lay outside her awareness. In her conscious waking life, she had no idea why she could not drink. Given that she subsequently recalled the apparent origin of the problem while in one of her absent states, we may infer the memory was there all along, only unconscious.

The division between conscious and unconscious functioning proved inadequate to capture the dynamic that became evident between the impulses we are led to repress – push from consciousness – and the forces that lead us to repress them and "resist" their reemergence. Both, it turns out, are unconscious. A system that distinguishes only unconscious and conscious processes cannot describe that opposition. Nor can it provide a basis for identifying the impetus to repress something, the judgment that an idea is dangerous, such that an operation to keep it from becoming conscious comes into play. Freud (1923) offers the taxonomy of id, ego, and superego to address those difficulties.

He reminds us not to conceive the terms too literally. Although he sometimes refers to them as agencies, they have no physical reality. They denote different forces in the mind, a status often forgotten in others' discussions of the scheme. Thus:

> *Id* refers to our unconscious impulses, both inherited and repressed, as they arise naturally, untainted by any external or intrapsychic influences.
>
> (Freud, 1923, p. 25)

> *Ego* embodies our striving to avert danger, whether from internal or external sources, and to maintain our bearings in the environment; it includes judgment, reasoning, and negation, elements of rational thinking and common sense.
>
> (Freud, 1923, p. 25)

> *Superego*, a differentiation that arises within the ego, observes the ego and judges it. Although its judging function

may make it seem rational and thus aligned with the ego, the judgments arise instantly and unthinkingly, driven, as Freud decided, by impulses of the id.

(Freud, 1923, p. 28ff)

The three interests, as we might call them, emerge in the sequence given, though, consistent with the idea that we always have some reality function, we always have some ego function: some monitoring of the environment and some adaptive response to it, like simple learning. But ego and superego develop – become more complicated – as we age, based on our experience and the way we assimilate it.

Distinctions within mental life along the lines of Freud's id and ego date at least to Plato, in the ideas of passion, or appetite (id), and reason (ego).[2] However, the idea of a superego is uniquely his, with the possible exception of Hume (1739), who believed self-appraisal is embedded in our emotional life. He identified what he called the "indirect" passions, feelings we experience that take the self or another as object. For instance, in the case of the self-oriented indirect passions, when we are proud, we feel good about ourselves, on account of some further characteristic of or connected with us – like our beautiful house – that causes us to feel pleased with ourselves.

Freud, however, is discussing an internal dynamic. The idea of a superego establishes the mind as more than its urges and passions – the id – and more than the thought and calculations that enable our everyday doings and the curbing of our passions – the ego. We also filter everything we do, think, and feel through a lens of self-appraisal.

We pass those judgments, largely unawares, on our impulses, acts, and thoughts. The judgements can have a harsh, punishing quality, the depth of which became clear to Freud in patients' psychoanalyses. Rather than cognize the substance of the judgments, we may feel an obscure remorse or guilt and strive, again largely outside awareness, to avert them. We may consciously experience their weight in the form of a general malaise or, in extreme cases, depression.

Freud fashioned a hypothesis about how the dispositions he calls the superego form based on conclusions he had come to regarding the forces he saw at work in patients' illnesses. The superego forms, according to him, from the Oedipal conflict that arises in the development of every individual. In its simple version, for boys, they yearn first for their mother and later also identify with their father. As their desires for their mother grow more intense, they perceive their father as an obstacle and want to eliminate and replace him. But because they also want to possess the father's privileges, they wish to be like him. They therefore continue to identify with him amidst the enmity they also feel. The relationship thus becomes ambivalent in that boys want both to identify with the father – to take him into the self – and to destroy him.

In the paradigmatic situation, the scenario plays out in the opposite manner for girls, who identify with their mother while desiring their father as a love object. However, the drama normally plays out to some degree in both directions for both girls and boys. All children desire more in their early life from both parents than they can give. We want total possession of them. Thus, we lust for both, find that each obstructs our aims regarding the other, and become jealous of each for the satisfactions he or she can attain that we cannot. As a result, we feel both love and hostility toward each and identify with each in our longing for the privileges we envy.

Eventually, in the process that will initiate the formation of a superego, children recognize their desires cannot be met and in the interest of survival repress them. They also, as a matter of course, begin to individuate from their parents, wanting some measure of autonomy while at the same time clinging to the dependency they have enjoyed until then. Both trends lead children to experience a loss of their parents. The loss prompts them to internalize, or *introject*, their parents as a means of retaining them.

Our first identifications, typically with our parents, last longest and have the profoundest effect on our character. They form the core of the superego, which assumes the special position the parents held for the child, as an ideal and an authority. In that position it embodies traits of the parents the child emulates, including the parents' repressive role against the child's Oedipal and other strivings.

In absorbing the repressive function, the superego assumes the parents' strength. But it also exceeds it. The harshness it comes to display exaggerates the power the parents actually wielded in the child's life. In both the course of *The Ego and the Id* and later writings (e.g., 1924, 1930), Freud develops a number of potential explanations for the exaggeration (see Chapter 8 here).

Both healthy and neurotic people struggle with the same conflict, Freud (1909a, Lecture V) says. It is the unavoidable result of being born human and influences all sectors of our mental life. Whether the struggle produces health or a neurosis depends on the relative strength of the forces in conflict and a person's inborn dispositions and accidental experience. A given instinct may prove stronger or weaker in one person than in another, or one person may turn out to be constitutionally more resilient than another in the face of similar environmental pressures (see also Freud, 1940, p. 185).

In his account of the superego, we see Freud's abiding commitment to the consequences and complexity of the development of the mind and at the same time its anchor in our origins. The superego encompasses the presumptive higher nature of humans, including morality, religion, and social feeling. Those institutions, as Freud explains across several works (e.g., Freud, 1923, 1930, 1939), arise, like the superego itself, from the most basic strata of our emotional life: from our Oedipal longing, our repression of those longings, and our internalizing of the parents and the authority they represent.

Freud, in that narrative, offers an alternative to the intuitive and predominant view that morality and religion, indeed all that is expected of our higher nature, arise from a lofty place in the human mind, or from God as the ultimate lofty place. His superego, as the continuation of the longing for the parents, or the father in particular, contains the seed from which religion evolved. Our judgment that we fall short of the internal ideal we have fashioned makes way for religious humility, to which believers appeal in their longing for the father, recast as a god. The tensions just noted between the demands of conscience – the superego – and our actual performance form the basis of guilt and hence of morality.[3,4]

Let us look more closely at the picture of moral sensibility he gives us. The imperative we feel when we think it morally right or morally wrong to do something exceeds mere knowledge of moral rules and the expectation of negative repercussions should we violate the rules. It reflects the legacy that gives us the superego: the love, animosity, and urgency we experienced at our parents' knees; the further hostility we turned back on ourselves for fear of abandonment by them; and the introjection of them that followed our relinquishment of any ambitions for total possession of them. We are moral not because we are innately endowed for it or because we learn to be so, but because we follow an inner compulsion that arises as a byproduct of our early emotional life and our inexorable development past it. It flows from our psychology, as cultivated by our experience.

Notes

1 This chapter tracks Freud (1923), *The Ego and the Id*.
2 Plato introduces a third area, spirit, which, however, does not survive into Aristotle's subsequent demarcation.

3 Social feeling, as it emanates from the superego arises from identifications we have made not with our parents but with peers or siblings toward whom we once felt rivalrous for the attentions of the parents or other authorities. The identifications replace hostile impulses we could not realize because of the repercussions they might have provoked, including the breakdown of the group (see Freud, 1921, for elaboration).

4 Freud, in the foregoing conceptualization of guilt and morality, converges with Nietzsche (1887, II), who also anchored them in our psychology, as a result of a torturous history of having to curb our instincts (see Chapter 8 here for additional elaboration of Freud's position).

Chapter 4

Revisions and Consolidation of the Theory[1]

Freud's tripartite schema for understanding our mental dynamics, like his delineation of basal instincts, intersects his idea of our operating in accordance with a pleasure principle. Id, ego, and superego represent different interests we try to satisfy. Their delineation also highlights the different conflicts that may arise among our strivings. The pleasure principle says only that we will press to satisfy the impulses we have, not which ones will prevail, which is the story of our psychological development and our disposition toward health or illness.

Although the pleasure principle remained the fundament of the psyche throughout Freud's writings, he eventually saw fit to modify it and reconceptualize its place in his larger framework. He discovered two exceptions to it, on account of which he modified, though did not profoundly alter, his theory. The first challenges the dominance of our striving for pleasure, and the second, Freud's understanding of what pleasure is.

An Exception to the Dominance of Pleasure Principle

There are many ways in which we may look like we are violating the pleasure principle when we are not. We sometimes endure pain for future gain, we have nightmares, and patients in treatment may sabotage their own progress, in what Freud terms the *negative therapeutic reaction* (Freud, 1923, p. 49). In

DOI: 10.4324/9781003394402-6

each such case, a payoff of some kind can be discerned: there is future, or more durable, gain; nightmares nonetheless fulfill a wish; patients sabotaging their treatment are enacting a wish to remain under care. Thus, those cases observe the pleasure principle.

But Freud could discern no payoff in the dreams of sufferers of traumatic neurosis. In those, the afflicted return relentlessly to the scene of the trauma – the shelling in the trenches, the train wreck, or any other profound shock that has generated their condition – and wake up in a terrific fright. Importantly, they gain nothing from the repetition, only more misery and more anxiety. Freud decided, in the light of such experiences, that although we repeat some painful experiences for benign ends, as when children repeat threatening experiences like a visit to the doctor's office in their play, we also may give way to a compulsion to repeat regardless of the outcome. The disregard of the outcome makes the compulsion independent of the pleasure principle. In the case of the recurrent dreams characteristic of traumatic neurosis, the compulsion to repeat suggests a system gone haywire, through a profound breach of its defenses (Freud, 1920).

Pleasure Redefined

Although Freud built his initial conception of pleasure around the prototype of the relief afforded by the discharging of excitation – as with an eyeblink – he came to see that we sometimes reap pleasure from an increase in stimulation; conversely, we may experience pain from a decrease in stimulation. For example, people enjoy sexual foreplay and masochistic practices, which increase excitation, and they can experience the agony of boredom from perpetual low stimulation. He determined that we derive pleasure from an alternation of peaks and valleys of excitation – as exhibited by the full arc encompassing sexual foreplay and the consummation of the sexual act, for instance – rather than from either a simple raising or simple lowering of it. He revised his definition of pleasure to include that rhythm (Freud, 1924).

Elaboration of the Theory

The two preceding developments – Freud's discovery of an apparent exception to the pleasure principle and his reconceptualization of pleasure – converged on an alteration in his theory.

In an avowed purely speculative excursion, he (Freud, 1920) followed out the implications of the compulsion to repeat for the composition of the most basic forces that govern mental life. For, even if the striving toward pleasure or away from pain, drives mental life for all intents and purposes, conceptually it is no longer the most primitive constituent of mental life, because some behavior, however rare, does not observe it.

He reasoned that all behavior we might call instinctual – that is triggered from within and follows a constant pattern – could be an instance of repetition compulsion. For instance, we have a nutritive instinct, set in motion by hunger, that always moves us toward the same result, namely satiety. Taking an even larger leap, he imagined that all of life may be an instinctual repetition on a grand scale. All life, no matter what happens in between, ends in death. It begins in nonexistence too, or it began from inorganic matter historically, and it ends there, as emblematized by "ashes to ashes." Thus, like traumatized soldiers returning in their dreams horrifically and to no apparent purpose to the trenches, life always ends up in the same place, the place from which it once emerged: inorganicity. Freud calls our natural, unavoidable drift in that direction the *death instinct*.

The use of the word "instinct" in the moniker "death instinct" is a bit misleading. It's not an active urge in the sense that are, say, the nutritive instinct, which presses us to find food, and the sexual instinct, which, in the canonical case, prods us to find a mate. Freud means it in a passive sense. He means a drift toward expiration, or, in our moment-to-moment doings, the drift toward no, or at least lower, stimulation.

In the light of the latter characterization, he labelled the ongoing expression of the drift the *Nirvana principle*, after the psychoanalyst Barbara Low (1920), or the *constancy principle*, after the psychophysicist Gustav Fechner (1873). Fechner found, consistent with Freud's (1911) notion that we trend toward reducing stimulation, that mental processes move toward a lowering of excitation or at least maintaining it at a constant level. Freud sees death as the ultimate realization of that tendency and identifies a death instinct on the grounds of that continuity. He means by it the tendency within us to let everything go, come apart, and, eventually, expire.

Once Freud (1920) identified a death instinct, though, he recognized that some force within us had to operate against it, or we would indeed die without having lived. He describes the opposite tendency as a clamoring for excitation, in the terms of what he metaphorically calls the life instincts or *Eros*. He sees in our sexual instincts that countervailing tendency in their pushing us, again canonically, toward the creation of new life. Hence the term *"life" instincts*.

But what balances out the death instinct in the individual – as opposed to the species – is the excitation our sexual impulses generate, not our drive toward reproduction. Only a tendency to raise the level of excitation could counteract the tendency to lower it. Just such an interaction occurs, Freud (1923, 1920) imagines, again highly speculatively, at our beginning. Rather than self-destruct – die – we aim the destructiveness ready to operate within outward, its active character produced by the active, energetic life instincts involved in turning it outward. It forms what will later become aggression once it finds an external object. Thus, we continue to live instead of imploding.

Though perhaps strange and less persuasive than other concepts of Freud's,[2] the transformation he envisions from the passive death instinct to the activity of aggression shows his commitment to determining what is most elemental in our psychology. It also makes clear that, contrary to popular representation of his theory, aggression was not a basic category for him. It involves the intermixing of the still more elemental life and death instincts. Nonetheless, he believed we have evolved by now to the point that the inclination to aggression is inborn in us (Freud, 1930; see Chapter 8 here).

Freud came to see most of our mental life as an "alloy," as he (Freud, 1923, p. 441) calls it, of the life and death instincts. The striving toward pleasure, still central in our psychological makeup, is one such hybrid product, a modification of the death instinct resulting from the incursion of the life instincts. It combines our lust after excitation and our longing for peace.

Freud's Theory: A Synthesis

Freud at the end of his career reached all the way back to the beginning of life in his continued search for the most basic principles of mental life. He identified there, respectively, an impulsion toward life and a drift toward quiescence, ultimately death, or inorganicity.

The individual mind, in parallel, strives toward the clamor of life and its tensions, on the one hand, and the release from tension and stimulus, on the other. The search for pleasure and retreat from pain – the "pleasure principle" – which Freud takes as a specifically psychological primitive, converges in part with that division. The striving for pleasure may incorporate both the attempt to reduce stimulus and the pursuit of it, while the attempt to avoid pain, or unpleasure, expresses the drive toward quiescence. Historically, we needed to make sure our pleasures were real, as opposed to illusory, and to adjust our aims in that light. We also need to monitor possible consequences of our intended actions and again modify our aims accordingly.

Within the envelope of the life and death instincts and more locally of the pleasure principle fit the day-to-day needs we satisfy, which Freud characterized as concerned most broadly with, respectively, sexual life and the preservation of self, or ego. The sexual instincts form around the prototype of reproduction, which produces new life and translates into various needs both closely and only distantly related to that function; thus, for instance, the category includes friendship, as well as physical manifestations of a sexual impulse. The ego instincts see to our individual survival. Both groups of needs set the pleasure principle in motion. When we experience the need of, say, hunger, pain and tension arise and ease only when the need achieves satisfaction.

Freud's final categories for distinguishing different interests and methods of operation in the mind include an id, ego, and superego. The id signifies pure impulse in the absence of any judgment or reflection. We wish, or want, only. The thinking self is embodied by the ego, which, in addition to wishing and wanting, judges, reasons, and monitors the external world. The superego, developed from our internalization of our parents and the drama therein, appraises the actions of the self, often harshly.

Our ongoing behavior and experience are the result of the joint action of all those strands of mentation. We rarely operate on pure impulse in our conscious waking life. We engage in thought and reflection too, judging and making choices. However, we seldom know all the motivations of our impulses. They are prompted by many influences, some inaccessible to consciousness. For instance, we might not know why, or entirely why, we want or like something or where a given thought came from.

When the different interests in our minds converge or when, in competition, they are able each to achieve at least partial expression, we enjoy a state of psychological health (Freud, 1909a, Lecture V). But it is inherent to human experience that that convergence occurs only some of the time. At other times, the interests of id and ego or superego may conflict. For example, a lustful or hostile urge (id) and a sense of propriety (superego) may conflict and lead us to recognize repercussions we cannot abide (ego). Conflicts within the ego may arise as well (Freud, 1940, Chapter VIII). When the poles of the conflict are unconscious, we can do little consciously to either unearth or ameliorate the conflict. Symptoms may erupt when the conflict becomes stronger than we can contain. Who will fall ill is complexly determined. Freud says both experience and constitution play a role, such that, for instance, of two people with the same life experience only one might develop a neurosis (Freud, 1940, p. 185).

Freud, in presenting the foregoing vision of our mental life, tried to isolate its most elemental constituents. He tried to demonstrate how from those elements the labyrinthine processes producing both mental illness and our highest intellectual and cultural achievements could grow.

In the next four chapters, we turn from Freud the theorist to Freud the observer. The two strands of inquiry developed alongside and informed one another throughout his career. They came together explicitly in some of his works, including *The Interpretation of Dreams* (1900) and *Civilization and Its Discontents* (1930), both of which we will review here in Chapters 6 and 8, respectively.

Notes

1 This chapter draws principally on two works of Freud's, *Beyond the Pleasure Principle,* 1920, and "The economic problem in masochism," 1924.
2 See Sugarman (2016, pp. 163–165) for discussion.

Part II

Empirical Inquiries

Chapter 5

Freud on Neuroses

The Case of Fräulein Elisabeth von R.

An intelligent and forthright young woman in good health has for a few years been experiencing crippling leg pains for no apparent reason. She can barely walk. It will fall to Freud to help her excavate the source of the life-diminishing condition and help restore her sanguinity (Breuer and Freud, 1895, case history 5).

Freud's treatment of the psychoneuroses represented his first psychological effort and the birth of psychoanalysis. This chapter examines his first complete analysis, involving a patient he called Fräulein Elisabeth von R. whose analysis he conducted in 1892. The case history is accessible and engaging, while at the same time methodical – and compact enough for us to review a good part of it here. It is above all sensitive, compassionate, and breathtakingly discerning. Tracing the analysis in modest detail, we can see how analyses, when pursued with care, can lead to sources of an illness and to the illness's resolution. We can see why Freud, and Breuer, would have concluded that some of our mental life occurs outside our awareness and how wishes, ideas, countervailing imperatives, and resistances all converge to produce our behavior.

Elisabeth von R., 24 at the start of treatment, had endured more than two years of pains in her legs and difficulty walking, which her referring doctor, finding no organic abnormality, thought might indicate hysteria. Her family had experienced great misfortune within just a few years: the death of her father,

DOI: 10.4324/9781003394402-8

serious eye surgery for her mother, and the death of a beloved married sister from heart disease. Freud, at their first meeting, found Elisabeth intelligent and mentally normal aside from her symptoms; she bore her adversities gracefully. He observed that she walked normally, despite her report of pain and fatigue in both walking and standing. The reported pain and fatigue were the only remarkable features about her he noted.

Diagnosis

Two comparisons led Freud to a tentative confirmation of the diagnosis of hysteria.

First were some purely descriptive considerations. Although people with organic pain tend to describe it calmly and in detail, Elisabeth gave indefinite descriptions. Additionally, people experiencing pain as part of other neuroses, like hypochondria or anxiety neurosis, give a sense of being engaged in a formidable intellectual task when they attempt to describe the pain: their features become strained and distorted, and their voices grow shrill as they struggle to express themselves aptly. Finding language inadequate to express the uniqueness of their sensations, they never tire of adding fresh details to their descriptions.

All the listed tendencies, accompanying neuroses other than hysteria, indicate a condition that has usurped sufferers' entire attention. Elisabeth's recounting of her pains showed the opposite tendency on every count. She described her condition calmly and nonchalantly and seemed content to relay it with dispatch. Freud concluded that, because she nonetheless attached importance to her symptoms, her attention must have been engaged with some other content, of which the pains were only an outward manifestation.

The second comparison suggesting hysteria concerns Elisabeth's response to the stimulation of her sensitive areas. People with organic pain show discomfort or wincing when their sensitive areas are stimulated. By contrast, when Freud pressed or pinched the sensitive areas of Elisabeth's legs, she assumed a peculiar expression, suggesting pleasure more than pain. She cried out, as though she were experiencing an erotic tickling sensation. She became flushed, threw her head back, shut her eyes, and bent her body backward. Although the movements were not exaggerated, they were noticeable. The accumulated reactions align more with an emotionally based than with an organic condition. The facial expressions in a case of hysteria would be assumed to connect to the content of the thoughts camouflaged by the pain, which the stimulation of the body parts associated with the thoughts had presumably aroused.

In the light of the two comparisons, Freud could find no explanation for the location of Elisabeth's sensitive zones, predominantly in her thighs. Based on additional considerations that arose later, he diagnosed an organic condition, a muscular rheumatism, that the neurosis hijacked, giving the organic condition exaggerated importance. Nonetheless, he began his treatment with physical interventions, mainly massage and electrical stimulation, which brought Elisabeth some relief, before launching the psychological therapy.

Freud proceeded in the treatment with just talking, rather than hypnosis, which he and Breuer had deployed until then. He believed Elisabeth had a conscious or near-conscious impression of the cause of her illness, which she was only withholding, by contrast with more usual cases of neuroses in which pathogenic material is repressed – inaccessible to awareness until the work of analysis is done. The talking method became his deliberate procedure in subsequent cases. The plan was to clear away pathogenic material layer by layer. Elisabeth would tell him what she knew, during which he would note the points at which she seemed to lose her train of thought or something seemed to be missing from it. He would then probe her memory at those points, using improvised procedures he describes as he recounts the case.

The Start of Treatment

Elisabeth first recounted her history through the period when her illness first developed, a wearying story, Freud says. The youngest of three girls, she had a close relationship with both her parents and, with her father, an intellectual camaraderie causing both parents to worry that her virility might scare off suitors. Her complete selflessness with family members led the parents to reconcile to her reduced femininity.

When her father fell ill with a previously unacknowledged heart problem, Elisabeth took the lead in nursing him for 18 months. Freud initially surmised that her neurosis dated to that period because she recalled having had leg pains that confined her to her bed for a day and a half during that time. She slept in her father's room otherwise, tending to him day and night and forcing herself to appear cheerful whether or not she felt it. She fell discernibly ill two years after her father's death, when, on account of the resurgence and intensification of her leg pains, she became unable to walk.

The year after her father died, the older of her two sisters married a gifted and ambitious man, whom Elisabeth disliked on account of his morbid sensitiveness and egoistic attention to his fads. She especially disparaged his lack of consideration for her mother, on which account he moved his family far away because of a promotion. But everyone welcomed the marriage of the second sister to a very considerate man, whose entrance into the family redeemed the idea of marriage for Elisabeth. Additionally, the couple remained in the neighborhood, which, among other advantages, provided Elisabeth with a nephew on whom she doted.

A difficult period followed when Elisabeth nursed her mother after eye surgery requiring her to be in the dark; Elisabeth was always with her. The three parts of the family reunited afterward for the summer holiday during which the others hoped Elisabeth would overcome the exhaustion and agitation she had felt while caring for her mother. However, it was during that holiday that Elisabeth's severe pains and locomotor difficulties began. Although she had noticed the pains' coming on sometime after the start of the visit, they came on violently toward the end. Because she had taken a long walk a few days earlier, it was easy to ascribe the pains to her having become overtired and then having caught a cold. She lived as an invalid from then on.

Later that summer, when she was away at a health spa with her mother, the two were called home because of the second sister's turn for the worse during a difficult second pregnancy. After an agonizing journey home, during which they expected the worst, they arrived to find the sister already lying in state. Elisabeth became possessed by the thought that a happy marriage, after finally materializing, was destroyed by a terrible end, which also devastated all she had hoped for as a benefit to her mother. Her brother-in-law, inconsolable after the loss, withdrew from his wife's family and returned to his own at their request; the two families judged it impractical for him to live with Elisabeth and her mother in the light of Elisabeth's being single.

Freud summarizes the story so far as the unhappy tale of a proud girl longing for love and embittered by the repeated defeat of her family and the loss of those she loved to death or estrangement. She found herself unprepared nonetheless to seek refuge in the love of an as yet unknown man. She lived in almost complete seclusion for the next 18 months, but for her care of her mother, and tormented by her own pains.

Nothing in the case history yet, Freud observes, explains why Elisabeth fell ill with hysteria or why she became ill when she did. Also of note, her telling of the story produced no salutary effect, unlike other patients' disclosures. The story was known to both Elisabeth and her family and, by itself, neither opened any new avenues of discovery nor precipitated any kind of catharsis. Her pains, meanwhile, remained as bad as ever.

Initial Progress: A First Conflict

In the light of his expectation that Elisabeth knew the causes of her symptoms, Freud asked her directly which event(s) coincided with the first emergence of her leg pains. Having found her insusceptible to hypnosis, which he had hoped to deploy as an aid, he used a maneuver he had developed for a different recalcitrant patient. He put his hand on her forehead and asked her to report whatever appeared to her mind at the moment of the contact.

After a silence Elisabeth described an evening on which a young man, a family acquaintance who had become a protégé of her father's, had accompanied her home from a party. She harbored the growing feeling, based on her contacts with him and remarks he had made to others, that he loved and understood her. She had started to think she might be able to tolerate marriage if it were with him, granted that he was not yet self-supporting, which meant she would have to wait for him.

Although she had experienced her most intense feelings for him that evening, she reproached herself bitterly, after she returned home to find her father suddenly gravely ill, for having spent the evening on her own enjoyment. She never left her father for an entire evening again and rarely met the man. After her father died, the man kept away out of respect for Elisabeth's grief. He eventually turned his attention elsewhere. The disappointment of that first love still distressed her whenever she thought of it.

Freud observes that Elisabeth's first pains coincided with a conflict that arose between the blissful feelings she enjoyed while in the company of the young man and the remorse she felt for that pleasure once she became aware of her father's condition. However, the pains appeared not to have become hysterical at that juncture, because they were mild and transient. Freud, now on the alert for other similar experiences, identified none during the period when Elisabeth was nursing her father.

Despite many subsequent attempts, he and Elisabeth found themselves unable to identify a psychical cause of the (intense) leg pains. Knowing now that the pains in at least milder form predated her blissful return from the party with her gentleman friend, he tentatively concluded that they represented a slight rheumatic disorder. The intense and abundant hysterical pains, which occurred later, simply made use of a preexisting condition that until then mainly eluded notice.

The treatment next entered a productive phase. Elisabeth surmised that the pains radiated from an area of her right thigh where her father would rest his leg every morning while she redid a bandage around it. Although she hadn't noticed the coupling until now, she felt sure it had occurred many times. Thus, the area had become a hysterogenic zone. Pain erupted there on account of a psychological association. It even began to respond to the therapeutic conversation. Usually Elisabeth experienced little pain when she and Freud began a session. But if a question, train of thought, or pressure to Elisabeth's head elicited an emotionally potent memory, a feeling of pain would arise. It was most often sharp enough that she would give a start and bring her hand to the spot. The pain would last while she remained under the influence of the memory. It would peak while she tried to describe the critical part of what had come to mind and would vanish at the end of the effort.

Freud adjusted their procedure accordingly. If Elisabeth reached the end of a description and still felt pain, he would prod her for more of the story until the pain had been talked away. Once they reached that juncture, she became susceptible to having a new memory evoked, in response to which they would follow the same procedure. During that period of what Freud, following Breuer's usage, called "abreaction" (Breuer and Freud, 1895, p. 149), Elizabeth's physical and mental condition improved to the point that she carried on without pain in her daily life most of the time.

At the same time, she experienced spontaneous fluctuations in her condition that, on inspection, turned out to be triggered by associations with contemporary experiences. For instance, she might hear of an acquaintance's illness that would remind her of her father's ailment, or a visit by her dead sister's child would stir up her grief. A letter from the distant, living sister showing the influence of the unfeeling brother-in-law brought on the pain, which lasted until Elisabeth had disclosed a family scene she had not yet mentioned. Because her symptoms were so easily aroused and then mitigated by such occurrences,

Freud began to further her encounter with situations likely to bring up provoking memories. For example, he encouraged her to visit her deceased sister's grave and to attend a party at which she might see the man she fancied when she was younger.

Memories from different eras would elicit the pain in different locations. Her right leg hurt when she discussed nursing her sick father, the young man, or other events that occurred during the first period of suspected pathogenic experiences. She would experience pain in her left leg when memories surfaced related to her dead sister or her two brothers-in-law, in other words from the later period of her illness. The disease thus seemed to differentiate into two distinct entities, one related to the nursing of her father and neighboring traumas and the other occupying the later period centering on her sisters and brothers-in-law.

Later Progress: A Second Conflict

Freud noted one particular episode from the second period, recalled vividly by Elisabeth, relating to the walk she went on when the three branches of the family – her two sisters' families and Elisabeth and her mother – were staying at a health resort. On the day of the walk, her mother remained behind, her older sister and brother-in-law had already left the establishment, and her younger sister, who felt ill, stayed in. Although initially the younger sister's husband was going to stay with his wife, he decided to join the walk at her urging on Elisabeth's account.

Elisabeth believed the walk coincided with the first appearance of her pronounced pains, which she recalled as having arisen acutely after the walk. Freud, responding to her uncertainty during the recounting about whether she had noticed the pains earlier, suggested that she might have refused the walk if her legs had hurt. Elisabeth, answering his query about a possible trigger for pain during the walk, remarked obscurely, according to him, the contrast between her loneliness and her sick sister's married happiness, of which the sister's husband's presence constantly reminded her.

In a related scene, which occurred a few days after the walk, after her (younger) sister and brother-in-law had left for home, she found herself in a restless, yearning mood. She rose early and climbed a small hill to a spot with a pretty view they had often visited together. Her thoughts as she sat on a stone bench there, she recollected, dwelled on her loneliness and the fate of her family. She admitted a burning wish to be as happy as her sister. She returned from the sojourn with violent leg pains, to which she succumbed long-term after her bath that evening. She was able, for a while after, to allay the pain by lying down until, when traveling home from the spa to see her ailing sister, she was tormented during the night by worry about the sister's condition as she lay sleepless, stretched out in a railway car.

Progress toward a resolution occurred after an obstruction arose in the analytic sessions. Although, in the first half of the treatment, Elisabeth freely came forward with memories when Freud pressed his hand to her head, she subsequently occasionally produced nothing. Though initially Freud curtailed the session, thinking the time unfavorable, he subsequently changed course. He noted that she often claimed nothing came to mind after she had spent a long interval during which her face showed a tense and preoccupied expression suggesting that she was grappling with content of some kind.

Prepared to assume for the sake of the analytic process that something came to her mind at such moments, he reminded her of the rule of treatment. She must remain completely objective and say what entered her mind when he placed his hand on her head, regardless of whether it was appropriate or honorable. To become free of her pains she would need to disclose everything. From then on, Elisabeth produced a memory or thought whenever Freud put his hand against her head. Sometimes he had to repeat the action a few times before she mentioned something; however, she would then admit that she could have said it the first time.

It is at this juncture that Freud introduces the concept "resistance," remarking that, in the course of his difficult work with

Elisabeth, he began to note the occasions on which her production of memories proved especially halting. During the ensuing period she made a productive effort in her treatment and enjoyed some mental relief. Nonetheless, her pains persisted, sometimes with their old severity. An incomplete result, Freud reasoned, indicated an incomplete analysis. They had yet to isolate when and why the intense pains had started.

Resolution

A chance occurrence led him to pursue a suspicion he had formed earlier. During one session, they heard Elisabeth's brother-in-law, the husband of the stricken sister, asking for Elisabeth in the outer room. She promptly rose and asked to end the session. Although she had felt no physical discomfort until then, her facial expression and gait now revealed the sudden emergence of pronounced pains. Freud bade her to reconsider the origin of the pains.

Her thoughts turned to the summer visit by the family to the health resort, now disclosing details of her experience that had not emerged before. For example, she had felt exhausted, including when on holiday, after having nursed her mother through her eye surgery and all the anxiety her mother's problem had aroused in her. She began to despair of ever getting any enjoyment out of life or achieving anything in it. Even though she had until then thought herself strong enough to manage without the help of a man, she now longed for a love in which – in her own words – her frozen nature might melt.

It was in that frame of mind that she had found herself deeply affected by her second sister's happy marriage: the loving care of the husband who looked after her, the way they understood each other at a moment's glance, and how sure they seemed of each other. On the walk that ended with Elisabeth's pains, which her sister had urged her husband to join on Elisabeth's behalf, she remained in his company throughout. They discussed all kinds of subjects, including intimate ones; she found herself agreeing with everything he said. The experience increased her wish to have a husband like him. The same wish returned a few days later when, after her sister and her family had left the resort, Elisabeth walked to the lookout that had been among the family's favorite destinations on their walks.

Although she felt pain when she stood up after her reverie there, the pain passed. It erupted again after her warm bath that evening and remained thereafter. When Freud asked her what she had thought of during the bath, she said only that the bath-house reminded her of her sister and her family, because their lodgings had been in the building. She continued to recall additional memories of the period: the subsequent holiday she took with her mother, the anxiety with which she waited for each letter from home, the news about her sister's decline, the train trip home in tormenting anticipation of what they would find there when they arrived.

She next recalled the last leg of the trip: the disillusioning impression given them by the relatives who met them at the train station; the short journey to her sister's neighborhood and their hurried walk through the garden; the silence and oppressive darkness within the house; the absence of her brother-in-law; and, finally, how she stood at the bedside of her beloved sister, who lay dead.

At the moment she admitted the terrible certainty that her sister had died without saying goodbye to them and without Elisabeth's having eased her final days with her care, another thought flashed through her mind and now bolted through it again. Her brother-in-law was free and could marry her.

The composition of the disease became clear. Elisabeth felt an affection for her brother-in-law that her entire moral being rejected. Her symptoms converted the unwanted psychical excitations into physical ones, as a result of which the unwanted thoughts disappeared from her conscious life. She succeeded, Freud summarizes, in sparing herself the painful recognition that she loved her sister's husband by inducing physical pains in herself. When the idea tried to force itself on her – on the walk with her brother-in-law, during her reverie at the lookout, in the bath, by her sister's deathbed – the pains assaulted her.

The broaching of that idea devastated Elisabeth, who erupted in terrible pains and tried to talk Freud out of the interpretation. He had talked her into it, she argued; it couldn't be true – she was incapable of such wickedness and could never forgive herself for it. It was easy, he says, to show her that her own narrative led to that conclusion. It took a long time, though, for her to accept his consolations: that we are not responsible for our feelings and that the fact that she fell ill attested strongly to her character.

Freud, faced with the task of alleviating her remaining suffering, now oriented the treatment around her relationship with her brother-in-law by helping her "abreact" the excitation she had built up in connection with it. Accordingly, they looked at the first impressions she had formed of his dealings with her, bringing her to recount all the little premonitory signs a fully grown passion can make much of when the bearer looks back on them. Those included his mistaking her for her sister on his first visit to the house and the sister's joking remark later when Elisabeth and her brother-in-law to-be had lost themselves in so animated a conversation that the sister felt moved to interrupt: "The truth is, you two would have suited each other splendidly." It gradually became clear to Elisabeth that her affection for her brother-in-law dated back a long time and had flourished under the mask of sisterly camaraderie, a natural sentiment for someone with the strong family feeling she harbored.

Elisabeth's mother, in whom Freud confided during that last phase of the treatment, had long suspected Elisabeth's fondness for her widowed brother-in-law. Many factors militated against a marriage between them, however. The brother-in-law had health issues and was having a difficult recovery from his wife's death. Freud and Elisabeth terminated her treatment when both believed she was progressing steadily toward a cure. After initially being angry with Freud for having shared her presumptive secret with her mother, she reconciled with him and recovered fully. She later married someone unknown to him.

Neuroses

It is difficult not to be struck, in the foregoing narrative, by Freud's shrewdness, sensitivity, and dedication as a clinician. There is his discerning assessment of the diagnosis of hysteria, followed by his canny observation of the clash between Elisabeth's first passion and her heartrending despair over the care she believed was due her father. Another pair of competing imperatives, between different directions of the heart as well as the call of propriety, dominates the later, full-fledged phase of the illness, though in the latter case the conflict raged unconsciously. We have, too, his keen observation of his patient: for example, how, when claiming nothing came to her mind, her face suggested someone hard at work internally. It seemed at least a good rule of thumb for him to assume she was so, because she came forth with productive material thereafter. Notice that he did not push her in a particular direction; he rather pointed out that something appeared to be occurring.

In this, his first complete analysis and the first in which he had his patient employ the conscious reflection he would later use exclusively, Freud and his patient worked meticulously to identify the thoughts to which her symptoms seemed to respond. She felt a deep attraction, unacknowledged, to her brother-in-law that, when it did surface, she found thoroughly abhorrent. Exposure of the conflict, combined with Elisabeth's negotiation of her feelings, coincided with the final disappearance of her symptoms and her return to full psychological health. The pattern parallels that of Anna O.'s treatment, discussed here at the start of Chapter 1. Recovery of what appear to have been the sources of her symptoms led to their extinction.

Many other cases Freud reports follow a similar trajectory, among them later ones involving neuroses other than hysteria.

In his celebrated "Rat Man" case (1909b), for instance, a young lieutenant suffered obsessive-compulsive symptoms, like chronic indecision and compulsive rituals to ward off thoughts he deemed dangerous, especially those concerning his father, some years deceased. As the patient, Paul, gradually retrieved and gave full expression to the ambivalence he had harbored toward his father and his ambivalence toward his romantic interest, his illness loosened its grip.

One such disclosure involved an episode from when he was between three and four in which he flew into a rage at his beloved father, who had beaten him on account of his having bitten someone. Lacking the standard terms of abuse, he screamed names of common objects at his father, while the beating was underway: "You lamp! You towel! You plate!" His father had stopped the punishment to say, "The child will be either a great man or a great criminal." Paul believed he became cowardly after the episode, afraid of his own fury (Freud, 1909b, pp. 205–206).

In all the case histories, the abating of the disease when the material to which the analysis led was brought forward supports the idea that the disease arose in the attempt to remove that material from consciousness. The disease, though debilitating, replaced the material with something less fearsome.

It was a bold insight of Freud's to think that the dynamic he and Breuer uncovered in the treatment of neurotics might generalize to other portions of mental life. The next three chapters examine that extension.

Chapter 6

Freud on Dreams[1]

Dreams have long fascinated people. Mystical speculation dating at least to antiquity saw them as messages sent from without, wanting only translation, whereas the science of Freud's day understood them as only the noise created by physiological processes.[2] *The Interpretation of Dreams*, the work that introduced him to a general audience and that he considered his cornerstone achievement, departs from both those views. A dream's substance carries meaning, according to Freud, *and* it comes from within the individual dreamer. It can be given an assignable place in our mental life. He does not mean by that only that the stuff of dreams comes from our minds. He means that there is a regular relationship between what appears explicitly in the dream and deeper currents of our thought, ideas that intersect essential concerns of our lives but are obscured for reasons he will extrapolate. It is the object of *The Interpretation of Dreams* to demonstrate that state of affairs and show how the work of making sense of a dream is done.

The central thesis of the book is that dreams, regardless of their outward appearance, fulfill wishes. They make an aspect of the dreamer's life more agreeable than it is in real life. The alignment of the thesis with the pleasure principle is obvious: dreams are making something better, according to Freud. In doing so, according to him, they parallel neurotic symptoms, which also provide relief.

DOI: 10.4324/9781003394402-9

Freud's Method of Interpreting Dreams[3]

The impetus for analyzing dreams came from Freud's early patients, who spontaneously described their dreams during their analytic sessions with him. It was but a short step from there to subject the dreams, rife with obscurity like the patients' symptoms, to the method of interpretation he and the patients were applying to the symptoms. Accordingly, Freud began to prompt patients to explore the thoughts and impressions that came to mind in connection with the dream imagery and the thoughts and impressions evoked by those thoughts and impressions, and so on.

Having patients reflect on one element of their dream at a time yielded richer and more productive results than did attempting to interpret the entire dream at once. Thus, a patient associating to a dream displaying a handkerchief strewn across a book followed by someone's lugging the table across the floor and into the garden would observe what came to mind, respectively, in connection with the handkerchief, book, table, table's movement, and garden. The patient might also consider the position of the handkerchief on the book.

Patients, as they did in their analyses in general, had to develop specific practices for the procedure to yield results. They had, above all, to pay close attention to the thoughts and impressions flowing through their minds so as not to miss anything happening there. To the same end, they had to eliminate any criticism or doubt of those contents and to relay anything that occurred to them, regardless of whether it struck them as irrelevant, meaningless, embarrassing, or offensive. Relaxation furthers both aims, by contrast with reasoning and reflection, which will reject some thoughts before the thinker fully perceives them. The ideal state, Freud believes, is the one we reach as we fall asleep, uninhibited but still able to report our thoughts.

The Interpretation of Dreams is densely populated by dreams and their analyses, the dreams coming mainly from two sources: Freud's own dreams, which he recorded upon waking and then subsequently analyzed; and his patients' dreams, as the patients reported them and then, with Freud, analyzed them. By the time he wrote the book, he had analyzed over 1000 of his patients' dreams, an additional indication of the wealth of material on which he bases his account.

He uses a dream of his own, the first among those he interpreted in detail (1900, p. 105), to illustrate his analytic technique and his convergence on the hypothesis that dreams fulfill wishes.

Freud's Dream of Irma's Injection[4]

Freud tells us, by way of preamble, that the dream occurred after he and his patient Irma had broken off her treatment for the summer, when, though she had made progress, she was not entirely cured, and they disagreed about the etiology of her illness. Earlier in the night during which the dream occurred, Freud had received a visit from his friend and colleague Otto, who, a friend as well of Irma's family and also her doctor, had come from visiting her family. He had told Freud that Irma appeared better than she had done, but not fully well. Freud reflected later that he had discerned a reproach in the comment that she remained unwell. He wrote out the case history that evening and had the dream overnight (p. 106). In the dream (paraphrasing),

> Freud, receiving guests in a large hall, encounters Irma and reproaches her for not having accepted his solution to her illness. He tells her that if she still gets pains, it's her fault. He also wonders whether she might not have an organic problem, given the nature of her complaints. Additionally, according to the dream, Otto had given her an injection shortly before whose composition was questionable, and the syringe was probably unclean.
>
> (p. 107)

Freud proceeds element by element to analyze the dream, down to the smallest detail, reporting the chain of associations he made to each constituent. He links each element with a recent experience and then prods the material further for additional lines of thought intersecting broader preoccupations of his. He recognizes that many of the elements, taken at face value, would exonerate him from any wrongdoing in Irma's care or would attest to his conscientiousness as a practitioner in general. To say that the illness could be her fault – because she would not accept his solution – would deflect the blame from him, as would the intrusion of an organic condition or an inappropriate injection given by Otto, not least with a dirty needle (pp. 108–118).

He resolves that the dream fulfilled desires – wishes – provoked in him by the evening's doings: Otto's remark that Irma was well though not fully cured, in which Freud heard a reproach, and his writing out of the case history, which he had hoped to share with a third colleague to justify himself (pp. 106, 118–120).

Were that narrative, of desires or interests fulfilled, to generalize to other dreams, then, Freud concludes, dreams would turn out both to have a meaning and specifically to fulfill wishes – to present circumstances the dreamer would be glad to encounter (p. 120).

Additional Dreams that Fulfill Wishes[5]

Additional dreams do appear to fulfill wishes, he finds, some explicitly. For example, he describes how he can make himself dream of bountiful drinking if he eats salty food, like anchovies, in the evening. The food makes him thirsty, and the dream sates the thirst. Such a dream not only shows a wish fulfilled, but in doing so, he thinks, serves the practical end of allowing him to sleep on, rather than waking to relieve his need. Freud calls it a dream of convenience (p. 125).

Additional instances include a recurrent dream of his in which, after working late into the night, he would dream, while struggling to wake, that he was up by his wash basin, thus obviating the need to get up. In an iconic dream of the type, a nephew of Breuer's, then a medical student and late riser, when called by name to wake ("Herr Rudi!"), saw a sign over a hospital bed, "Rudolf Kaufmann." He told himself he needn't get up because he was already in the hospital (pp. 125–126).

Children dream the simplest of the transparent dreams of wish-fulfillment. Freud's daughter Anna, at 19 months, when denied food during the day due to illness, called in her sleep, "Anna Fweud, stwawbewwies, wild stwawbewwies, omblet, pudden!" Other children Freud mentions likewise dreamt of missed treats or of excursions they had looked forward to but were denied. Anna, at 8½, dreamt that a 12-year-old boy she liked was one of the family (pp. 127–131).

Folklore and language recognize dreams as wish-fulfilling, Freud observes. "What do geese dream of?" "Of maize," according to one of many similar sayings. And we declare, "I would never have dreamed that!" or "Not in your dreams [might that happen]!" (pp. 131–132).

Dreams that Fulfill Wishes Despite Contrary Appearances[6]

Even when we experience dreams as anything but wish-fulfilling – when they frighten or displease us, for example – they still may be fulfilling a wish or serving a positive purpose, Freud found. The wish-fulfillment becomes evident when we consider the thoughts to which dreamers' analysis of their dreams leads them (pp. 134–135).

For instance, it is not immediately obvious that Freud's dream of Irma's injection fulfills a wish. In the dream's explicit, or manifest, content, he was giving a party attended by, among others, Irma and some of his colleagues. The doctors, on examining Irma, noticed some abnormalities. They entertained a handful of explanations: an organic condition, a dirty needle, and so on. It was only on analyzing the dream – examining the thoughts that came to mind in connection with the dream's elements – that Freud came to understand the dream as divesting him of responsibility for the persistence of Irma's disorder (p. 136).

Why, he wonders, on the assumption that the dream arose to express that implication, would it not simply have presented him outright with the affirmation of his professional stature? After all, some dreams express their wishes directly: his wish for water when thirsty; Rudi's wish to sleep on rather than wake to go to work at the hospital; children's wishes for missed treats and abandoned excursions.

To answer the question, Freud examines another dream of his that, like his dream of Irma's injection, has an ostensibly indifferent surface. Dreams with more charged surface content, like those arousing fright, raise additional issues, which he considers later.

Freud's Dream of the Uncle with the Yellow Beard

In the dream, an image appeared of his friend R's face drawn out lengthwise and surrounded by a yellow beard. He understood that R was his uncle and that he felt great affection for him (p. 137).

He gives as background to the dream two professors' recommendation, shortly before he had the dream, that he be promoted to professor extraordinarius, an eminent post the rough equivalent of assistant professor in the English-American system. Although the news heartened him, he had resigned himself to the likelihood that he would not succeed, because he knew of equally qualified colleagues who had been denied. Earlier in the evening, he had received a visit from one of those colleagues,

R, who had just learned that his being Jewish had put him at a disadvantage, a disadvantage Freud shared.

The dream easily appears indifferent on the surface. It contains an image of the face of an acquaintance, along with the assertion that the image is someone else. It is also obscure. Why would R's face be elongated and surrounded by a yellow beard? Why would he be Freud's uncle, and why the great fondness for him?

However, Freud's analytic process, rather than respond directly to questions such as those, begins simply with dreamers' observing as effortlessly as possible the associations brought to mind by individual dream elements. Let us follow him briefly as he begins the process with the dream of the bearded uncle.

Turning to the ascription that R was his uncle, he has the immediate thought that he had only one uncle, a derelict in the eyes of the family. The man, eager to make money, had participated in an illegal stratagem for which he had been caught and punished. Freud's father, anguished by the event, said later that the uncle wasn't so much a bad man as he was a simpleton. Freud, now pondering the connection the dream established between R and the uncle, infers that the dream presented R as a simpleton, an imputation he found untrue and disturbing. He notes separately that he, in fact, had five uncles, some he admired and held dear. However, because his waking memory had at first fixed on just the one objectionable character, he assumes that one to have been the intended one (p. 138, 138n).

Freud, contemplating the fair beard, recalled that R's beard, originally dark, had begun to turn gray, transitioning, as Freud's own beard was doing, from black to reddish brown, to yellowish brown, and finally to gray. That detail further established the face in the dream as R's.

Why should the dream have made R out to be a simpleton, not to mention a criminal? R was upstanding, except for the time he was fined for having knocked down a boy with his

(R's) bicycle, a trivial comparison. But now Freud recalled a conversation he had had a few days earlier with a different colleague, N, who, like Freud and R, had been nominated for the professorship, but was then turned down, apparently, like R, on account of his being Jewish. When N subsequently congratulated Freud on his (Freud's) nomination, Freud dismissed the encouragement on the grounds that he suffered the same drawback. N had answered jokingly that, whereas a woman had once started legal proceedings against him in a bald attempt at blackmail, Freud had an unblemished record (p. 139).

How the Dream Fulfilled a Wish

Freud now supposed that the dream was showing him how, despite the count against him, that he was Jewish, he might yet earn the promotion. The coupling of R with Freud's uncle went to show that R was a simpleton, while N, of whom Freud was reminded by the imagery and its subject, was a criminal. Although Freud might have shared their denomination, they had other drawbacks that would surely have cost them the advancement. Therefore, Freud had a chance (pp. 139–140).

Thus, as happened in his dream of Irma's injection, a bizarre and even unsettling state of affairs in the dream – the prospect of organic illness and a faulty injection in Irma's case and the defamation of his friend (R) in the dream of the bearded uncle – allowed a separate wish to be fulfilled. Had Irma suffered an organic illness or received a faulty injection from someone other than Freud (namely, Otto), then Freud was not responsible for her imperfect recovery, and his professional reputation remained intact. Were R a simpleton and N a criminal, then Freud, who shared their religion and not the other demerits, might have a chance at the professorship. The effusion he felt for the uncle/R figure in the dream, he concludes several steps later in his analysis, tempered the distaste he felt for slandering R in the dream, for depicting him as a simpleton.

Important at this juncture in Freud's developing account is, on the one hand, that dreams with indifferent and even unsettling content can be understood as having a positive purpose and, on the other hand, that such content may appear in distorted form. Neither the Irma dream nor the dream of the bearded uncle is transparently wish-fulfilling in the way a child's dream of missed strawberries would be.

Now Freud wonders why, if dreams that don't look beneficent on the surface nonetheless fulfill wishes, they don't simply present their wishes outright. In a beneficent rendering, Freud, instead of dreaming of Irma's injection, would have been depicted directly as responsible and respected, and, instead of finding himself presented with the bearded R as his uncle, would have found himself on a path toward the vaunted promotion. Adults, he answers, do not readily admit to the wishes they satisfy in dreams. The waking, rational Freud would not expressly linger over a wish to be regarded as having no responsibility in Irma's imperfect condition or a wish to be grand and respected. Likewise, he would, and did, demur when given the news of his nomination for the promotion to professor extraordinarius.

Dreams, Freud concludes for now, are shaped by two forces, wish-fulfillment, on the one hand, and censorship, on the other. One process constructs the wish the dream will satisfy, and the other censors and distorts the expression of the wish, making it acceptable to the mind that will perceive it. Censorship is thereby a process that allows content to enter consciousness.

Consciousness, Freud extrapolates further, is a quality ideas acquire through a specific psychical act. The act – censorship and distortion in the case we're discussing – is separate from the process of forming the idea. Thus, in Freud's telling, his wish in the dream of the bearded uncle to persuade himself of his prospects for promotion despite his friends' lack of success reached his consciousness, via censorship and distortion, as an image of something else. The wish was one thing and the obstruction and resulting deformation of it something else. Consciousness, in that view, is a sense organ that perceives data that form elsewhere, given appropriate manipulation of the data. It does not create the data; it is an attribute that may attach to them (p. 144, also pp. 615–617).

Distressing Dreams

The dreams Freud has considered so far had at most mildly disturbing content, like the prospect that Irma might suffer an organic disease, that he thinks either allowed another wish to be fulfilled or else distorted it. What of more pointedly distressing dreams, which present us with circumstances we *don't* want? He ventures that those, also, disguise a wish, specifically by fulfilling a second wish, to block the expression of the first wish. In that way we end up both wishing and denying the wish, satisfying both impulses in a way that ordinary waking life normally doesn't let us do.

Freud's patients, usually skeptical of the theory that dreams, no matter their content, invariably fulfill wishes, lustily challenged the theory by reporting dreams they believed contradicted it. But, with the patients' help, he identified wish-fulfillment within the dreams.

In one dream, for example, a woman patient dreamt that, though she wanted to give a supper party, she had only a little smoked salmon in the house. Thinking she would go out to buy provisions, she recalled that it was Sunday, and the shops were closed. When she next attempted to contact caterers, she discovered her phone was out of order. She abandoned the plan and hence denied her wish to hold a supper party (p. 147).

The woman, in response to Freud's prodding her for the events of the previous day, related, after evident resistance, that she had visited a friend of whom she felt jealous because her husband often extolled the friend. The patient expressed relief, though, that the woman was very slender, whereas her husband prefers a more robust figure. In response to Freud's subsequently asking what the two talked about during the visit, the patient mentioned the friend's wish to grow heavier.

Additionally, the friend had asked, fondly, when she might next be invited to share another meal with the patient and her husband, who always fed people well (p. 148).

Freud, with that information, extrapolated a tentative solution to the dream, which he now perceived denied one wish to fulfill another. By denying herself the dinner party, the patient accomplished the aim of not giving the friend the opportunity to grow stout, thus diminishing the threat the friend posed to the patient's favor with her husband. To test his speculation, he asked the patient what the significance might have been of the smoked salmon, the one food she had on hand. Smoked salmon, she replied, was the friend's favorite dish (p. 148).

In a similar case, a young doctor who had submitted his honestly completed tax return showing his spare earnings dreamt that the government was fining him severely for underreporting his income. The dream, though expressly distressing, nonetheless implied that he was a doctor with a large income (p. 157).

Other distressing dreams, Freud has found, either satisfy a masochistic streak the dreamer has or, in the case of anxiety dreams, or nightmares, defend the dreamer against another wish. In the case of the masochistic streak, the dreamer wants to suffer; thus, a desire is fulfilled. In the case of nightmares, the defense Freud believes they embody may take different forms: it may distract the dreamer from the dangerous wish or distort it, or it may punish the dreamer for having it. Regardless of the precise means, a second aim beside the original wish is being fulfilled – to deny the original wish (pp. 157–159).

Freud is modelling the foregoing conception of anxiety dreams on the profile of neurotic anxiety. In neurotic anxiety in, say, a phobia, a surface fear, for instance of open spaces (agoraphobia), or of a particular animal like dogs or horses, masks a deeper terror so far concealed. The object of the surface fear, though frightening, can at least be escaped from, whereas the deeper fear cannot be. Correspondingly, he wants to argue, the terror of anxiety dreams applies only superficially to the manifest imagery. It arises from a concealed threat generated by the dream's initiating wish (pp. 160–161).

Freud's aim at this juncture is only to make it plausible that dreams that don't appear to fulfill wishes, and may even appear to do the opposite, may nonetheless fulfill wishes. The wishes, which are not apparent, may require either suffering or the denial of another wish for their fulfillment (pp. 160–161).

Distortion is the process by which he envisions the concealed wishes he's now assuming to exist present in the explicit content we experience. As such, he concludes, the explicit content materializes as a product of censorship. We censor wishes that confront us with a danger or other undesired result that prompts us to recoil from satisfying the wish. The distorted fulfillment of a wish effects a compromise in that we both satisfy the wish and conceal it from ourselves.

Freud's Later Chapters

The chapters of *The Interpretation of Dreams* we have reviewed so far, Freud's Chapters II-IV, form the core of the argument of his book. According to that argument, dreams can be inserted into our waking mental life through a process of interpretation that draws on our retrieval of memories and summoning of other impressions inspired by the individual elements of the dream. When we follow that process as far as possible and integrate its threads, we can identify a wish, or more than one, the dream has fulfilled: a scenario we would be happy to encounter, though to which we as mature adults would likely not admit. Accordingly, Freud posits, a distortion changes the fulfillment into unobjectionable and usually baffling form.

The remainder of Freud's treatise builds on that core without materially changing it. He uses the foregoing propositions to explain why dreams favor the type of content they do (his Chapter V) and then how the presumptive wishes dreams fulfill are transformed into the content we experience (his Chapter VI). Then, in his final chapter, he situates his theory of dreaming in a general psychological theory of the mind, which achieves its first full articulation there (his Chapter VII).[7]

The general theory, which he reiterates in his 1911 paper "Formulations on two principles in mental functioning" and modified throughout the remainder of his career (see Chapters 1 and 4 here), holds that all our mental processes observe a pleasure principle. They trend away from what will cause us discomfort and toward what will bring relief or pleasure.[8] That we follow that rubric means that we do what we do for a reason.

As Freud illustrates in his "Two principles" paper, that understanding of our motivational makeup is what undergirds psychoanalytic therapy. Behavior that strikes the observer, as well as the patient, as pointless, counterproductive, and even painful may be serving another purpose that isn't evident. It is that dynamic that holds the behavior in place. Once patients discover the concealed purpose, the grip of the behavior on them loosens. The big step Freud took in his work with dreams was to determine that dreams, like neurotic symptoms, even if bizarre and distressing, make something better: they fulfill a wish as he conceptualizes it.[9]

The Interpretation of Dreams

The Interpretation of Dreams was a breakthrough work. It presented the idea that unconscious mental processes take place in all people, not only those who fall ill, and that occurrences as common as dreams can provide a point of departure for excavating some of those processes.

Also evident in the hundreds of pages of dream analyses in the work is the potential for dream analysis to penetrate areas of our mental life that might not come to light otherwise. Because dreams occur when the editing and organizational activities of consciousness are shut down, elements may appear in dreams that would not penetrate conscious waking life. Those elements, in turn, can prompt memories and lines of thought during waking analysis that might not otherwise emerge. A good example of that effect can be found in Freud's (1918) "Wolf Man" case history, in which a dream – about wolves – the (adult) patient recalled from his childhood eventually prompted recollections whose retrieval led to his cure. That revelatory potential of dreams gives substance to Freud's famous characterization that the interpretation of dreams offers a "royal road to a knowledge of the unconscious activities of the mind" (1900, p. 608).

When dreams are plumbed for purposes akin to those that might emerge in the treatment of a neurosis, their analysis opens pathways to dreamers' inner thoughts and indeed their wishes.[10] To that extent, Freud has given us a productive analogy and dramatically widened the scope of his inquiry.

Notes

1   This chapter traces the argument of *The Interpretation of Dreams* (Freud, 1900). The arc of the argument is unaffected by Freud's later writing on dreams, except as noted (note 9, this chapter).
2   Modern neuroscience has enlarged the picture of the neural underpinnings of dreaming, which some think are incapable of supporting dream structure as complex as the sort Freud posits (e.g., Domhoff, 2019; Hobson, 1988), whereas others perceive a compatibility (e.g., Solms and Turnbull, 2007). As the diversity of opinion suggests, the neural data cannot decide the psychological question. That is especially the case given the widespread misimpression among modern writers that Freud's psychology of dreaming is complex. He believed dreaming a strikingly primitive mental process, by contrast with waking thought.
3   As per Chapter II of Freud (1900).
4   Though discussions abound in the literature of Freud's interpretation of this and other dreams he reports, I am taking him at his word regarding his understanding of this and other dreams I consider here. My aim is to show how his analyses proceeded, for which purpose we need accept only that the trains of thought his reflections elicit could plausibly have been active in his mind. I weigh elsewhere (Sugarman, 2023) the likelihood that the dream materialized from those thoughts.
5   Per Chapter III of (Freud, 1900).
6   Per Chapter IV of Freud (1900).
7   Although some of the concepts he discusses appear in his earlier unpublished "Project for a Scientific Psychology" (1895), the earlier work couches the theory in neural terms, which Freud had rejected by the time he wrote *The Interpretation of Dreams*.

8 The second principle he discusses in the 1911 paper is the reality principle, which holds that we develop toward making sure that our satisfactions are real and enduring, so we don't end up suffering later. That principle fine-tunes the pleasure principle, rather than standing outside it.

9 Freud, in later revisions of the general theory, recognized a limiting condition on the pleasure principle, as discussed in Chapter 1 here. The mind can be overwhelmed by stimuli, as in a case of trauma, in which event its defenses are so severely breached that it cannot even strive to reduce pain, let alone cultivate pleasure. When such breaches occur, it may fall victim to patterns that violate the pleasure principle (Freud, 1920 and Chapter 4 here). But for all intents and purposes, the pleasure principle rules our mental life, as Freud concluded in *The Interpretation of Dreams*.

10 Whether that means that they, like neurotic symptoms, originate in the conflicts and frustrations to which their analysis leads is less clear, as I discuss in Sugarman (2023).

Chapter 7

Freud on Ordinary Waking Mental Life

Freud, though known mainly for his treatment of the psycho-neuroses and his theory of dreams, also wrote on fragments of ordinary waking mental life. The best known of those investigations is his account of so-called parapraxes, small, transient mental errors, like slips of the tongue: you say one thing when you meant to say another. An error, however, is an aberration of a process, just as dreaming and psychoneurotic symptoms can be seen as deviations from ordinary waking mentation. Freud also tried his hand at analyzing waking happenings that are not aberrant, but simply part of our regular doings. Those include making a joke and appreciating humor, getting lost in a book, and the experience of the uncanny, among others.

This chapter looks at Freud's examination of such subjects. The investigative tools at his disposal are more limited in those instances than they are in his investigations of dreams and neuroses. In the case of dreams and neuroses, he drew on lengthy analyses of the experiencer: dreamers, including himself, in the case of dreams and patients in analysis in the case of neuroses. Although he utilizes similar contextual observation for a few occurrences of parapraxes, his accounts of ordinary waking life otherwise draw on common experience and a theoretical analysis of it. His tactic in most cases is to show that the phenomenon he is trying to explain would be difficult to account for unless mechanisms along the lines he proposes were operating.

DOI: 10.4324/9781003394402-10

It is with reference especially to his analysis of parapraxes that Freud is sometimes referred to pejoratively as having overinterpreted behavior. Some so-called Freudian slips seem perfectly innocent, containing just a phonetic mix-up and no hidden meaning. Freud was aware of happenings requiring no special explanation. The occurrences that caught his attention and of which we will observe a sampling here were specifically those on which he thought he might productively bring to bear his ideas of more complex dynamics. The other behaviors and experiences we will consider, although also common, elude straightforward explanation. It is in that explanatory crack that Freud's apparatus has something to offer.

Three of the topics Freud considered follow, beginning with parapraxes, his examination of which he gathered into a single volume, titled *The Psychopathology of Everyday Life* and published in 1901, a year after *The Interpretation of Dreams* appeared.[1]

Parapraxes

Here is an example from *The Psychopathology of Everyday Life*, involving a slip of the tongue.

Freud describes a patient to whom he had suggested, based on their immediately preceding conversation, that she had felt ashamed of her family during the period they were discussing and had reproached her father with an insult she had so far not disclosed. She claimed she recalled no such occurrence and thought it unlikely. She continued the interchange with the remark: "One thing must be granted [the family]: they are certainly unusual people, they all possess *Geiz* (greed) – I meant to say *Geist* (cleverness)." The allegation of greed expressed the reproach Freud had suspected she had held back (Freud, 1901, p. 64).

The disturbance of speech evident in a slip of the tongue can, as Freud himself points out, arise simply from mechanical interference like the assonance between the intended word and another similar one or the anticipation of words or sounds to come later in the sentence (Freud, 1901, p. 56), as in "Can we turn on the heat seater [viz. seat heater]?" Such interference can become disposed by states of fatigue or divided attention or under the influence of disturbing emotion (Freud, 1891, p. 13). However, a verbal slip can also arise from influences outside the intended word or sentence, influences of whose existence the utterer becomes aware only through the occurrence of the error. Freud suspected the latter possibility in the case of his patient.

Although it remains possible that phonic similarity and a moment of inattention accounted for the patient's error, it is a plausible alternative story he tells. The motivation for substituting *greed* in the sentence existed, in both the immediate context – Freud's voicing of his suspicions about the patient's low opinion of her family – and the so far-unacknowledged thoughts of hers that had been hinted at in the analysis.

Freud's explanation of parapraxes – including many beyond slips of the tongue like the forgetting of proper names, the mislaying of objects, and more – engages a kind of wish-fulfillment or at least a purpose, as neurotic symptoms and dreams do, according to him. In the case of a parapraxis, an unconscious intention allegedly intrudes on intended currents of thought to create a structure that realizes the intention. In the case of a slip of the tongue in particular, when we fall into uttering a word we didn't intend, we sometimes have an interest in saying it or in what it says. In the case of the forgetting of names, Freud demonstrates in an instance of his own how an interfering intention, to forget a deeply painful memory possibly aroused by the conversation he was engaged in, might have disrupted his recovery of a name he knew well (Freud, 1901, chapter 1; Sugarman, 2023, Chapter 6).

Parapraxes, like neurotic symptoms, involve a disruption of ordinary (waking) activity that calls for accounting. Freud suggests that competing intentions may interfere with the activity, producing the incongruity, and, where he has contextual information, shows how the interference might happen – granted that some occurrences involve lower-level errors like phonic anticipation. When neurotic symptoms arise, the root of the interference lies deeper and is ongoing and more stubborn. When we dream, on the other hand, our minds give us a nightly experience different from what we entertain in waking life. Nothing is disrupted. It is simply a different form of mental activity that needs to be explained. Freud thinks that something akin to a clash of imperatives is occurring nonetheless – between the wish seeking expression and the considerations that would lead us to deny the wish.

Jokes and the Appreciation of the Comic

You might not think the production and appreciation of the comical requires any special explanation. Something funny happens, like the telling of an uproarious joke, and we laugh. But there is more to it than meets the eye. What makes a joke funny? And why do we laugh in response to them, that is, why is it laughing that we do? Why don't we sigh or cry or turn around in a circle?

The account Freud offers in his *Jokes and Their Relation to the Unconscious* (1905b) addresses those questions. Although the volume eventually considers the broad class of the comic extending beyond jokes, his investigation centers on jokes, as we will do here.[2] Jokes, especially ones over 100 years old, though perhaps less intuitively engaging than the broader class of the comic in general, make up a rich and well-defined set of phenomena that admit of progressive step by step analysis. Freud handily implements just such an analysis in a methodical, masterly treatise, second in length among his works to only *The Interpretation of Dreams*. Synopsized excerpts from the text follow, constructed to highlight his method of investigation and the psychological explanation he constructs.

Joke Techniques, or, What's So Funny?

As ordinary hearers, we would have a difficult time distinguishing what we are laughing at when we laugh at a joke. Jokes typically convey some content encased within a particular form. If someone asked us, when we laugh, which of those, content or form, we were laughing at, we wouldn't have a clear intuition about the answer. The whole package seems funny. Freud begins his investigation of jokes with a systematic examination of the relative contribution of jokes' form and content to the creation of the resulting humor.

He uses an elegantly simple test he calls a method of "reduction." He rephrases known jokes into a direct statement of their meaning and judges whether the humor remains. Thus, he translates the joke, "I drove with him *tête-à-bête*," into "I drove with X *tête-à-tête*, and X is a stupid ass." The latter, literal, statement of the joke's meaning scarcely raises a laugh. That tells us that the form of the joke is what makes it funny.

We can also see that only a small maneuver makes the form what it is and accomplishes a compression of the meaning into a shorter form than is needed to articulate the meaning literally. The mere replacement of the *t* in the second *tête* by the b of *bête* allows the two terms to be combined into one and avoids the entire assertion of "*il est un bête.*"

The joke, therefore, through that maneuver, "condenses" its content in two ways: the collapsing of the two assertions into one of the same length as either of the original ones ("I drove with X *tête-à-tête*, and X is a stupid ass" becomes "I drove with him *tête-à-bête*"), and the merging of two words into one, again, with no gain in length (the second mention of *tête* in *tête-à-tête* becomes *bête* by the replacement of the initial *t* with *b*). Freud calls the whole process "condensation accompanied by slight modification" and ventures that the slighter the modification, the more satisfying the joke (Freud, 1905b, p. 25).

After reducing a long series of jokes in the same fashion, Freud delineates additional techniques of joke construction that involve plays on words, as the *tête-à-bête* example does. Double entendres, which utilize the different meanings of the same single word or phrase are an example. One can be seen in the courtier's reply to Louis XV's demand to have a joke made of which the king was the subject (*sujet*): *Le Roi n'est pas sujet* ("The king is not a subject") (Freud, 1905b, p. 37).

A large category of jokes makes use of conceptual, rather than verbal, play, some of those relying only on subverted logic and not on wording per se. Paraphrasing Freud's example:

> A man in a pastry shop who had ordered a cake returned it uneaten and asked for a liqueur. He drank it and began to leave without having paid. The proprietor, intercepting him, asked him to pay, upon which the man said, "But I gave you the cake in exchange for it." The proprietor: "You didn't pay for that either." The man: "But I hadn't eaten it."
>
> (Freud, 1905b, p. 60)

Freud teases out, tests, and codifies the techniques that appear to operate in such specimens as well.

He ends the first, analytical part of his study with a delineation of the characteristics sufficient to produce jokes. He believes himself to have sampled the possibilities broadly enough to have extracted the most common and most essential techniques. Those, he thinks, all converge on a psychological economization, or a saving in psychological effort, of some sort – for instance, a compression of words or ideas (or both) or play in place of serious thought. Now the question becomes what the connection is between the resulting economization and the generation of pleasure.

The Purposes of Jokes and the Production of Pleasure

Preparatory to that inquiry, Freud divides jokes into two groups according to whether they carry any kind of invective, as many do. One group, innocent jokes, does not do so and aims only to produce pleasure in the hearer. An example would be the Italian-language joke *Traduttore-Traditore!* Translators are traitors (to the language), but the idea is meant as a jest, rather than as an attack, granted Freud's caveat that jokes thoroughly innocent of any ulterior purpose may appear only in childhood (Freud, 1905b, p. 132). The second group, tendentious jokes, carries a potentially offensive message of a hostile, obscene, cynical, or skeptical sort. "I drove with him *tête-à-bête*" is an example. It carries an insult and hence hostility.

Freud observes that tendentious jokes tend to elicit more intense pleasure in their hearers than do innocent ones. Their more pronounced effect makes them a good point of entry into the question of how pleasure comes to be generated in a joke of either kind. Again enlisting his method of reduction, he shows how tendentious jokes always cloak their potentially offending content in an allusion. For example, "I drove with him *tête-à-bête*" implies, rather than asserts, that the subject of the joke is a stupid ass. The pleasure of the joke may come in part, therefore, from the recognition of the allusion: from the recognition of the illicit content under the protective cloak of the ellipsis.

Why might recognition of that presentation give rise to pleasure? We would normally inhibit acknowledgment or enjoyment of the risqué content we are on the verge of appreciating, and that inhibition requires psychical effort on our part, Freud begins. It takes work to inhibit the flow of mental activity in the direction in which it wants to go. On the other hand, if an inhibition can be made unnecessary, then the energy we would have expended on it is saved. Tendentious jokes, in only alluding to the offensive content, make the inhibition unnecessary and save us the energy we would have spent erecting or maintaining the inhibition. The yield of pleasure, Freud proposes, corresponds to the psychical exertion prepared and then saved.

He thinks that innocent jokes, though they lack the illicit content of tendentious jokes, might prompt a different sort of saving in psychical expenditure. The pleasure in those seems to derive entirely from the form of the joke, which, as he demonstrated with the *tête-à-bête* joke, is a primary source of the humor of all jokes.

Some jokes, for instance, involve a kind of word play, in which sound is emphasized over meaning. After a host served a *roulard* (or *roulade*), a labor-intensive preparation, a guest asked whether the delicacy had been made in the house. The host replied, "Yes, indeed. A home-roulard," exploiting the phonetic similarity between otherwise unrelated items of politics (home *rule*) and cooking (roulade). Similarly with other types of pleasure in nonsense, like faulty thinking and absurdity; we economize on psychical effort in relaxing the rules of disciplined thought.

In another group we recognize something familiar. A joke from Lichtenberg (cited in Freud, 1905b, p. 82) repeats and then subverts an adage: "It is almost impossible to carry the torch of truth through a crowd without singeing someone's beard." Although the joke projects a bit of invective, we get some of our pleasure from the play of the familiar – carrying the torch of truth – in it. The discovery of the familiar, in turn, Freud says, saves the effort we might expend in processing something new and has a delight all its own (p. 122).

The foregoing joke techniques share another property Freud thinks is also integral to the economization on psychical work he believes they effect. They each embody a characteristic of childhood mentation and thus a further saving in psychological expenditure by shedding from us the burden imposed by subsequent development. The linking of words through sound at the expense of meaning dots children's early word learning and word play. To capitalize on the rediscovery of the familiar recalls the signature childhood pastime of thriving on repetition and deriving intense pleasure from it (Freud, 1920, p. 7). Babies shake their rattles or enjoy someone else's funny faces over and over again. Children like to hear the same story, or repeat the same game, many more times than adult interest would sustain (Freud, 1905b, p. 122).

If joking techniques spare us psychical expenditure and thereby give us pleasure, then we can see how tendentious jokes confer greater pleasure than do innocent ones. Because tendentious jokes use the same techniques as innocent ones do and add their own source of economization – we are spared the effort of inhibition against the illicit content – they must yield greater pleasure (Freud, 1905b, p. 135).

Why We Laugh at What's Funny

We come to the critical test of any theory of jokes: why we laugh at them, that is, why it is laughing we do. Freud has surmised so far that the object of joking is enjoyment, and the source of the enjoyment is the savings of energy afforded by both the release from inhibition and the mental work we save through our assimilation of the joke techniques. The question remains of how it comes about that laughter is the specific result that occurs.

Two factors need accounting. First, laughter is a pleasurable response of a particular kind, an explosive discharge, by contrast with the more measured release of, say, a sigh, which can also indicate relief from an exertion of some kind and the accession to pleasure. Why is the outcome laughter? Second, the laughter that arises in connection with joking occurs not, or not so much, in the teller of the joke, but in the hearer. The explanation of the latter effect provides leverage on the explanation of the former: the occurrence of laughter as the result of a (successful) joke.

Suppose, as a first approximation, the laughter has something to do with the lifting of an inhibition suddenly found unnecessary, as Freud has already suggested. It must be that both the teller and hearer of the joke have been spared the inhibition. We may assume from the resulting laughter that the hearer has let go of the inhibition. The teller must have had it lifted as well: were the tellers of jokes to experience no lifting of inhibition, they could not generate the joke. The difference between them must arise instead in the possibilities for discharge of the effort neither needs any longer.

So, Freud surmises, the production of the joke must itself attenuate the energy available to the teller for discharge. Hearers, meanwhile, receive the joke ready-made. As long as they need no extra effort to comprehend the joke, and the joke succeeds in beginning to spur the relevant inhibition in them, then their inhibition will become superfluous the moment it forms. It is caught *in statu nascendi*, as Freud calls it (Freud, 1905b, p. 151), borrowing the term from Gerard Heymans (1896), who used it somewhat differently in his theory of the comic. The hearer, in Freud's conception, then "laughs off" the extra "quota" of energy, in much the way our arm flies into the air when we lift something we expected to be heavier than it is (p. 149).

The Involvement of the Unconscious in Jokes

Freud suspects joking engages a process different from that involved in our ordinary discourse, specifically unconscious manipulation. Although we speak of "making" a joke, our behavior differs from what we do when we "make" a judgment or create something. A joke, when we come up with one, seems to arise in us involuntarily. It is not that we know ahead of time the joke we are going to produce, and all we need to do is find words for it. Instead, Freud says, we have an indefinite feeling coupled with an *absence* – the blank state that precedes slipping into a hypnoid state he talks about in reference to his early case histories (see Chapter 1 here) – and a sudden release of intellectual tension; then suddenly the joke arrives, typically already clothed in words (Freud, 1905b, p. 167).

By contrast, we have a choice with other intellectual maneuvers. We can decide to make an allusion. For instance, we might want to share a thought whose direct expression might produce unwanted effects. We decide, on that account, to frame the point more delicately and indirectly, via an allusion. In that case the allusion is a figure of speech and not a joke. It remains under constant supervision by our ongoing thought, by contrast with the unmonitored sudden popping out of a spontaneous joke that happens to make use of an allusion (Freud, 1905b, pp. 167–168).

The idea that, when we form a joke, our ongoing thought gets subjected to unconscious processing, evokes for Freud a parallel to dreaming. Indeed, he discerns many superficial similarities between the joke techniques he has described and the "dream-work" he portrays in *The Interpretation of Dreams*; the dream-work is the process through which the thoughts and wishes that form the dream's substance, according to Freud, are transformed into the dream's outward form. Both, for instance, appear to exhibit condensation. The joke, "I drove with him *tête-à-bête*" collapses two assertions into one, according to Freud's analysis. Dreams, once they are analyzed, appear to compress many trains of thought into a limited surface form, the dream of the uncle with the yellow beard (see Chapter 6 here) a case in point. In both he sees a return to the methods of child mentation and play, the signature mark of the unconscious (Freud, 1905b, p. 165; see Chapter 3 here).

The Contribution of the Jokes Study

Freud's meticulous deconstruction of joking is a model of psychological inquiry, at least through his consideration of why we laugh; his comparison of joking and dreaming is more speculative. He takes a spontaneously occurring piece of human behavior and peels it back layer by layer with shrewd analysis. Although we may not know whether he has identified exactly why laughing is what we do when the mental funny bone is tickled, he shows us the work an account must do.

Getting Lost in a Story[3]

Producing parapraxes and cracking jokes are things we *do*. Imagine instead becoming totally transported by a novel you are reading to the point that you are hanging on every word, unable to put the volume down. True, you are doing the reading, but something happening *to* you makes you keep going. Freud believes that that experience, no less than our committing parapraxes or making and appreciating humor, contains more than meets the eye. Why do strings of words on a page concerning individuals we don't know and who don't even exist keep us turning the pages to find out what happens to them? To conceive that circumstance, he (Freud, 1908a) asks us to imagine tracts we would nowadays call B novels, light plots that engage our fancy and keep us reading. What makes that adhesion possible?

Straightforward answers may come to mind. We relate to the characters, or they present a new world that entices us. Perhaps the writer dots the narrative with teasers about what lies ahead and deftly dangles one cliffhanger after another.

Explanations like those fall short. That we can relate to the characters – empathize with or find ourselves in them, for example – might explain why we might be interested in them, but not why we would stay up half the night clinging madly to the story. Clever manipulation of the narrative also does not explain either why we so readily abandon our own world and totally inhabit another or the narcosis we feel when we do so.

Even writers themselves, the instigators of that narcosis, cannot say how they make that impression on us, Freud observes. Accordingly, he launches a search for the source, first of the writer's activity and then of its effect on the reader, with the identification of something we all do that resembles the writer's craft. He pinpoints imaginative activity as that occupation and traces its origin in our development to children's play. Both creative writers and children at play fashion a world according to their fancy. They take that world seriously, investing it with great emotion, while at the same time distinguishing it from reality.

As we age, we exchange playing for daydreaming, in which we continue to invent happenings shaped by our fancy and fueled by our emotions, abandoning only the connection of the make-believe to tangible objects. However, although children happily expose their play to onlookers, adults conceal their fantasies. Children's play, Freud explains, realizes their wish to be grown up, which they have no reason to hide. Adults' daydreams fulfill unsatisfied erotic and ambitious wishes, to which they would be loath to admit.

A typical adult daydream, Freud illustrates, might unfold in the fantasy of a man on his way to inquire about a job: He might imagine getting the job, impressing his employer, becoming indispensable in the firm, being welcomed into the employer's family, marrying his lovely daughter, and eventually running the business. To Freud, the sequence reproduces the protecting house, loving parents, and first love objects of childhood, all projected onto an adult vision of the future using the objects of the present.

The same ingredients populate the B novel. The hero manages to survive and triumph despite adversity, his success sufficiently assured that we read along securely, while his invincibility attests to the bald egoism of the story. Additionally, all the desirable women in the tale fall in love with him, thus realizing the fantasy's erotic side. Although many narratives depart from that model, Freud believes we could link even major deviations from it to the same template through intermediate cases.[4]

Writers' narratives, he suggests, originate in the writers' own wishful fantasies anchored in the same template. However, those narratives, unlike the daydreams of ordinary non-writers, which would evoke only disinterest or disgust in their audience, entice readers with carefully designed disguises and formal aspects of composition that form the writer's gift.

Thus captivated by what Freud calls the incentive bonus of the text, we readers, he concludes, proceed to reap our deepest pleasure from the release of preexisting tensions in our minds. Those tensions are formed of our basic erotic and ambitious

wishes, the ones our daydreams fulfill. They now find fulfillment, then reemergence, then fulfillment again, and so on as we
are carried along by the writer's art.

The process, then, is tantamount to daydreaming, indeed *is*
daydreaming, which explains why we continue onward, una-
ware of anything else and unable to let go. Although the writer's
talent may keep us going with cleverly placed suspense, it is the
underlying gratification that allows the suspense to work.

Becoming swept up in a story, put into a state of fascina-
tion by it, though ordinary, is more complicated than it might
seem. Though many surface-level features we might point to –
like the relatability of the characters, the lure of the familiar,
the shock of the unfamiliar – might prompt our interest in an
offering, some integral piece of our psychology must answer
to and power us through it. Freud says such narratives arouse
our most basic wishes, typically erotic and ambitious ones, and
offer the prospect of their fulfillment. In our captivation with
those tracts, we are daydreaming. Daydreams seem to fulfill the
same wishes and occur because we have the wishes.

In trying to understand the magic reading fiction produces
on us, Freud relies not on close analysis – as in the case of
jokes – but on common observation. Most of us get lost in
books. There's a type of writing, the B novel, that especially
disposes us to that effect. The standard B novel follows such-
and-such a course. In doing so it resembles daydreams. Perhaps, like them, it gratifies basic longings of ours. A threat to
the fulfillment of those longings would keep us reading; their
attainment, at last, would warm our hearts and make us eager to
repeat the experience.

This is not depth psychology. It is ordinary looking combined with methodical reasoning, seasoned by a mind accustomed to looking at behavior and asking what makes it go

Ordinary Waking Mental Life

Freud's analyses of additional waking mental phenomena of
ordinary life produce results like the three preceding ones of

parapraxes, joking, and getting lost in a book, respectively. They include experiences like the feeling of the uncanny (Freud, 1919), the pangs of mourning (Freud, 1916, 1917a), and the paradoxical surprise people sometimes feel when coming face-to-face with something they knew existed but had never seen (Freud, 1936).

Regardless of whether we are ultimately persuaded by any given account, Freud builds a compelling case, through methodical examination of the experiences and alternative explanations, that explanations that do the work his do are needed.

The further revelation of Freud's treatment of ordinary mental life is that there is a way to analyze it that connects it to essential trends in our minds – in everybody's mind. Looking at particular pieces of ordinary experience and behavior, he identifies an anomaly – something unexplained, like why we laugh at a joke or go into a trance when we read – and goes about systematically solving it. He shows a deft hand with that identification, not only finding an anomaly where others might not do so, but finding one that will lead to a stratum of our psychology that feels generative of the behavior that results.

Notes

1 I have examined at length elsewhere (Sugarman, 2010, 2023) Freud's treatment of the phenomena covered in this chapter.
2 I restrict my coverage to Freud's treatment of jokes to expose his reasoning most clearly. I treat his analysis of other instances of the comic in Sugarman (2010).
3 This section draws on "Creative writers and daydreaming" (Freud, 1908a).
4 Freud offers a somewhat different account of the pleasurable effect of tragedies and other stories with distressing content (e.g., 1906).

Chapter 8

Freud on Civilization and Society[1]

How do we manage to live in groups, in which one person's happiness could easily be another's pain?

Freud, as early as the 1910s, extended his inquiries beyond the individual mind and the contemporary moment to the societal and the historical. The pinnacle of that work is *Civilization and Its Discontents* (1930). In it he weighs the priorities of the individual life against those of the group and wonders how both the group and the individual psyche formed in the first place and evolved to be what they are today.

He is not the first to have tried to extrapolate to the origins and metamorphosis of the human psyche and its place in the group. Antecedents include Hobbes, Rousseau, and Nietzsche, each narrating, as Freud does, a speculative tale at once based in observations of contemporary social life and meant to echo it.[2] Freud diverges from the others in drawing on an articulated vision of our individual psychology, a synopsis of which appears in Part I here. In this chapter we will watch him extend that understanding to the societal palette, while fine-tuning and expanding the general vision to address the crossroads civilization had reached by the time he wrote.

Pursuing Happiness

If our behavior is driven by the pleasure principle – we seek relief from discomfort and cultivate pleasure when

DOI: 10.4324/9781003394402-11

possible – then why are we so bad at fulfilling it? The pursuit of happiness infuses all we do. Such is the program of the pleasure principle, which prods us toward the removal of pain and the cultivation of pleasure. That program cannot succeed, Freud says, given both our constitution and the world we live in. We achieve happiness in the strictest sense from the satisfaction of needs dammed up to a high degree, as exemplified by sexual life. That type of satisfaction necessarily arises only episodically. We achieve at most mild contentment from any desirable situation that is prolonged. At the same time, we suffer easily, on account of our bodies, the external world, and our relations with other people.

Given those limitations on our prospects, we moderate our claims to happiness and mostly try not to suffer too much. We have developed many means for the latter, including withdrawing from the world, chemically altering our being for instance with alcohol, engaging illusion like that offered by art, and the enjoyment of beauty. Some of the methods, like the enjoyment of art or other found beauty, induce at most a mild narcosis, in Freud's telling, a temporary withdrawal from our needs. Yet we prize them highly and would be loath to do without them. Some seek solace in religion, which Freud (1927, 1930) finds a limiting and dangerous choice because of its anchor in illusion and submission.

Though we will never achieve the happiness we strive for, we will not abandon the pursuit of it. Freud wants to understand the forces that so profoundly impede us.

Civilization and Its Demands on the Mind

Our decision to live in groups – our civilization, in other words – may be decisive in undermining our path to happiness, though we rightly cherish it. The impingements of the external physical environment and of our bodies, which are inevitably headed for disrepair and decay, though challenging, are less debilitating mentally.

Living in groups requires regulations that manage human relations, so that the will of the group is always stronger than the will of any individual. Justice would have come about, Freud imagines, to ensure that laws once created would not be broken on any individual's behalf. The development of civilization, therefore, would necessarily have constrained individual freedom, in particular the satisfaction of our instinctual needs.

The satisfaction of our instincts, as we saw in Chapter 2 and as Freud reminds us here, is the "economic task of our lives" (Freud, 1930, p. 96); he means by "economic task" that to which we devote our efforts. He notes three mechanisms by which humans have come to alter their instinctual dispositions to meet the societal demand.

One is through the fixing of some instinctual impulses into *character traits*, like parsimony and the concern with order and cleanliness. Those traits, when exaggerated in neurotic patients, appear, based on the patients' analyses, to express displaced anal eroticism,[3] which Freud assumes occurs in the milder and more general case as well.

A second means by which instincts alter when they meet an obstacle is through *sublimation*. Through that mechanism an impulse is redirected to a new aim by means of which it can discharge safely. A toddler's penchant to gaze at and try to explore others' bodies may become replaced later by a curiosity and inquisitiveness about things in general. Freud thinks the higher achievements of civilization – like art, science, and the construction of ideology – may have come about similarly, through a long series of sublimations of primitive instincts into workarounds of greater propriety.

The third and most drastic transformation of instinct is the blanket *renunciation* of it, in other words the outright denial of satisfaction. A child ceases to look and to explore, eventually repressing the urge to do either. Even the first two mechanisms – the formation of character traits and the mobilization of sublimation – block full satisfaction of the targeted instincts.

But we would not naturally deny our instincts satisfaction. The denial must come at a cost and in doing so crucially compromise our mental life. On account of that renunciation of instinct, people become hostile to civilization, a hostility that itself exacts a toll on them. Freud progressively illustrates both costs in the remainder of *Civilization and Its Discontents*.

Critical to that itinerary, as with all of Freud's undertakings, is the internal nature of the kind of account he is seeking. His will not be a litany of external events that occurred to which humans responded. It will be a narrative of how the mind digested and adapted to its circumstances. Even where he tells a just-so story of given events to anchor his vision, as he will do next, the thread we are to follow is that of the implications for the mind. The importance of recognizing that motif goes beyond easing our comprehension of his text. Freud is frequently disparaged for failing to take account of the environment in which the development mind finds itself. The criticism is misplaced. His aim is to describe how the mind works.

How Civilization Began

Freud, looking to understand the psychological forces that might have allowed civilization to form, offers as a first approximation that civilization was founded in love and necessity. Love encouraged the formation of the family, to assure individuals of ongoing sexual satisfaction and protection for their young. Necessity, or the matters vital to survival, heightened primal humans' sensitivity to the advantages of work in common. After discovering they could improve their lot through work, they could have perceived the further benefit of the combined efforts of many.

However, love and necessity, Freud resolves, would be insufficient alone to hold the wider community together. Love, although the origin of civilization, he believes, would also have conflicted with it. The family would have wanted to hold onto its individual members, which would have acted to draw them away from the community. Severe restrictions imposed by civilization on sexuality further attest to a conflict between them.

As for necessity, common interest, which necessity spawns, would not suffice to draw members back out to the community. Among the reasons, groups inevitably generate their own tensions, seen in in-fighting, for example. Additionally, although the advantages of work in common would seem ideally suited to encourage collective effort, it does little to incite unity. Most people disparage, rather than embrace, work (Freud, 1930, p. 80n1, also p. 75). Something else must bring together people who are not connected by family.

The Puzzle of the Incitement to Universal Love

In his search for an additional incentive, Freud reflects on the doctrine of universal love. We are asked to love not only those close to us, but all people. Why? Why might civilization make that demand?

The doctrine is odd, he finds, when we view it from a detached perspective. When we love indiscriminately, as the doctrine asks us to do, we devalue the love we feel for our own people, he says. The adjunct precept that we should love our neighbor as ourselves is equally dubious. Our neighbor, who shows us no consideration or, worse, hurts or exploits us, might instead deserve our enmity. The incongruity reminds Freud of the defense mechanism of *reaction-formation* in which people compensate for impulses of theirs they fear with exaggerated expressions of their opposite. For example, a wife who loathes her husband may gush with solicitude for him, solicitude she doesn't feel and whose artificiality she may betray by exaggeration.

Aggressive urges such as those, thoroughly inconsistent with universal love and which exist within every human – it is those, in addition to the inevitable conflict between individual and community, that threaten to erode our relations with our neighbors. People are incited to bond with one another, Freud concludes, to neutralize aggressive impulses that would otherwise destroy society. Nonetheless, that incitement has added little toward realizing universal love. Humans cannot give up aggression. Because civilization requires the restriction of the sexual and aggressive impulsions humans naturally harbor, people find it difficult to be happy in civilization.

Aggression in Freud's Theory of Instincts

What is aggression that it is so inevitable and immutable a part of us? We saw in Chapter 4 that it is not a basic instinct in either Freud's earlier or later typology of instincts. When he had, at first, conceived as the most elemental instincts only the sexual and ego, or survival, instincts, he did not even consider aggression except in the form of sadism, which he understood then narrowly as a manifestation of sexual impulsion (Freud, 1915; see Chapter 2 here). Later, after delineating the still more elemental life and death instincts (Freud, 1920), he came to see aggression as a mixture of the two, a view he elaborates most fully in *Civilization and Its Discontents* (1930).

His idea in that later view is that our most basic, irreducible tendencies are toward the buildup and discharge of excitation. The sexual, or more broadly life, instincts embody the accrual of excitation, and the death instinct its diminution and ultimately elimination. Aggression, resulting in the destruction of things, connotes death, accounting for Freud's ascription of it to the death instinct. But aggression is active too and, in Freud's conception, therefore engages the life instincts as well.

Freud, by the time he wrote *Civilization and Its Discontents*, was increasingly struck by the existence and ubiquity of nonerotic forms of aggression, exemplified most profoundly by war and the buildup to it. He thus deemed it reasonable to stipulate a free-standing, inborn inclination in humans toward aggression. Even then, he still believed the inclination to be always alloyed in some degree with the life instincts. Aggression incorporates an assertion of omnipotence, he says, a sentiment allied with narcissism, hence sexuality and therefore life (Freud, 1930, Chapter VI; 1940, Chapter II). With aggression being inevitable, the question presses of how we rein it in, to the extent we do.

Guilt as a Barrier Against Aggression

The doctrine of universal love is just that, a doctrine – an exhortation to love all our fellow humans – not an assertion of what we naturally do. The command is clearly insufficient; examples of its violation abound. Although we also have laws and regulations, those would hardly contain the subtler forms of aggression – like surreptitiously undermining a peer at work – of which even the most law-abiding citizens are capable. Civilization must have evolved other means to keep us in check.

What it has evolved is guilt, which controls our impulses from within. Guilt, according to Freud, is aggression, combined with a corresponding need for punishment, turned inward toward the self. It can arise regardless of whether we have carried out the deed or betrayed the sentiment that precipitates the guilt or whether we have only contemplated it. That internal constraint on our aggressive impulses is what compromises our psychological life, producing the malaise Freud perceives permeates humankind, on account of which the title, *Civilization and Its Discontents*.

A theorist needn't be psychoanalytically disposed to conceive guilt in that way. Nietzsche resolved, while psychoanalysis was in its infancy and not yet concerned with matters of culture and history, that guilt and other lofty moral sentiments had brutal origins. Much as Freud would argue later, Nietzsche (1887) imagined that humans, forced to purge their impulses for the sake of so-called civilized society, directed the animosity aroused by the curtailment against themselves. Trapped, they beat themselves rather than the outer world that foisted the new life on them. Freud's next tries to map out the way our individual development disposes that result.

How We Develop the Capacity for Guilt

To experience guilt we need, first of all, to conceive a given act or impulse as bad. We are not born with a sense of good and bad. We learn those values from our caregivers. Left to our own devices, we would distinguish only the agreeable and the painful, as per the pleasure principle.[4]

We first understand as bad acts that might threaten the loss of love; we avoid those acts to avert that threat. People's mentality at that juncture is more social anxiety than a guilty conscience. Their morality extends no further than their fear of punishment and their efforts to avoid it. It is the only morality available to children. It is not until we undergo the development Freud describes as the formation of the superego, which results in the internalization of the parents (see Chapter 3 here),[5] that we attain conscience proper. We reproach ourselves for our intentions, judge our actions before we execute them, and punish ourselves accordingly.

The idea that intentions, and not only acts, can incite the reproaches of conscience finds support, Freud maintains, in the reproaches that fully abstemious people, like celibate clerics, can suffer. The temptation, for example to aggress, increases the more it is held back and the savagery of the attack on self – the self-reproach – increases in kind.

Thus, to inhibit an impulse toward, say, aggression at the behest of conscience – the superego – is to provoke one act of aggression while restraining another. We exchange our outward aggressive impulse for an inward-directed one in the form of harsh judgment and retributive battery. Even if in doing so we gain the love or approbation of the authorities, we do so at the price of internal unhappiness.

The Severity of the Superego

If the reprisal of the superego increases from the withholding of given impulses – let us say aggressive ones for now – then the severity of the superego depends on factors beyond the severity of the original model, the parents. Were the severity of the superego merely imitating the severity of the parents, or even an exaggerated vision of that severity people might have formed in childhood, then we might expect the severity of the superego to diminish over time. It does not do so; it may even increase, if, for example, every aggressive impulse we feel but restrain leads to fresh self-reproaches and doubts.

Freud thinks, in the light of analyses of neurotic patients, who suffer especially brutal self-reproaches, that something like that occurs. Later, in his posthumously published *An Outline of Psychoanalysis* (1940, p. 150), he remarks people's tendency to tear their hair or beat their face in some moments of intense exasperation. He imagines that they are leveling against themselves the treatment they wanted to deliver to someone else.

Maybe, Freud reasons further, the superego – the tendency toward severe self-appraisal and battery – directs against people the hostility they wanted to hurl at the authorities who foiled their earliest and hence strongest impulsions. They withheld the animosity out of fear of loss of love, the animosity that now comes back at them.

Why Only Frustrated Aggression Becomes Guilt

Having illustrated how inhibited aggression can become guilt, Freud asks whether guilt might arise from the inhibition of other instinctual impulses, as other psychoanalysts of his day believed it does. He thinks guilt forms from the inhibition only of aggression. Only aggression provides the impulsion of which guilt is made, namely aggression directed inward.

Frustrated erotic demands, he remarks, would not supply that impulsion. Those demands, for instance unrequited lust for a parent or sexual needs left unfulfilled by a spouse, would produce only unspent libido, which is to say sexual energy with nowhere to go. By themselves they would not generate a current of aggression that could then turn back on the self.

Nonetheless, frustrated erotic urges could provoke aggressive impulses, for instance against the spouse, which, if withheld, could turn into guilt.

Still, unfulfilled erotic demands would not simply lie dormant. They can appear as neurotic symptoms. Freud long observed in treating patients that neurotic symptoms express unfulfilled erotic wishes. A canonical case appears in his *Introductory Lectures on Psychoanalysis* (1917b, Lecture 17, pp. 261–263), in which an obsessive patient followed the same ritual each morning of rushing from her room to an adjoining one, where she stood by a table and summoned her maid. She then either sent the maid on a trivial errand or dismissed her, while she returned to her room.

Analysis revealed that she was re-enacting the scene of her wedding night, on which her husband had proved impotent after running from his room to hers several times to try again. When the patient ran to the table during her ritual, she always stood next to a large stain on the tablecloth, which her maid would have to have seen when answering the patient's call. Her ritual corrected the scene of her wedding night, leaving on the supposed bed sheet (the tablecloth) evidence that what didn't happen (consummation) did occur and allowing the maid to see it. The symptom had a sense, as Freud would say, and improved the patient's circumstances, as per his understanding of the work symptoms do.

The Future of Civilization

Freud has no intention of passing any final pronouncement on civilization, which after all is constantly evolving, save to say that, though it is much to be prized, is not wholly good. After addressing parallels and differences between individual development and the trajectory of civilization, he expresses concern about two dangers threatening the well-being of both individuals and civilization. One is the ubiquity and ferocity of external aggression, which was on the increase at the time with the steady march toward World War II. The other is the persistence of guilt, a scourge on both people's happiness and their ability to go about their lives.

He wonders whether further development will prove able to master the disturbance created by both inward and outward aggression. At the time he wrote, the human race had developed the capability to destroy itself, which he thought may have contributed to the unrest, anxiety, and unhappiness he saw. He wonders whether, moved by the life instincts, we would be able to tip the balance back the other way.

Freud's Widened Compass

Society is riddled with aggression, greed, and deception, with their consequence of great suffering and resignation, and is yet capable of love, laughter, and breathtaking accomplishment. In *Civilization and Its Discontents*, Freud tries to explain that juxtaposition: the impasse we find ourselves in of simultaneously yearning for, and erecting obstacles to, both individual and societal peace and happiness

He engages the pleasure principle – the attempted payoff he sees all our internal processes and external actions striving toward – in the way the striving for pleasure is classically understood, namely *as* a striving. We try to be happy. When he speaks in other works of our conformity to the pleasure principle, he alludes more to how our behavior falls into line with it. We naturally act so as to avoid pain or repeat paths known to bring relief or pleasure. Those may not be the express aims we have in mind. They are rather a guiding principle that underlies what we do have in mind.

The search for happiness is but a starting point for *Civilization and Its Discontents*, which concerns itself mainly with the self-generated ways in which we are not happy, via the guilt that directs our would-be aggression back against us. The guilt is not something we actively seek. It is something – something painful – that arises within us as we try to avert another threat.

Freud, throughout the work, deftly applies his understanding of the development of the individual psyche to the direction of humanity as a whole and uses the reflection on society to enrich his notion of the individual. He understands both as the modification of organic life brought about by the exigencies of reality, or necessity, given our decision to live in groups. We must curtail that which is inborn in us, to live together. Both the wondrous and less fortunate achievements of which we and the culture around us are capable reflect the history of the accommodations thus made.

Notes

1 This chapter centers on *Civilization and Its Discontents* (Freud, 1930).
2 See: Hobbes, *Leviathan* (1651); Rousseau, *Discourse on Inequality* (1755); Nietzsche, *The Genealogy of Morals*, Essay II (1887).
3 Anal eroticism is a normal phase of development people ordinarily surmount naturally, whereas the overcoming of neurotic fixations requires intervention, usually therapy (Freud, 1908b, also 1909a, p. 44).
4 Freud, in his paper on Negation (1925), writes that the first good/bad distinction we make is between what we want to take into the self and what we want to push away. Only later do we become concerned with concepts like true and false, good and bad in any moral sense, or, as per his "Two principles" paper (1911), real and not real (see Chapter 1 here; also, Sugarman [2016], Chapters 2, 6, and 11).
5 The superego forms from the resolution of the Oedipus complex, as described in Chapter 3 here. We take the parents into the self as we relinquish our aspirations with respect to them, the internalization the natural response to losing them as the objects we envisioned they were; we experience their loss also as they pull away from the near-symbiotic relation they had with us earlier and as we pull away from them in our striving toward greater autonomy.

Essential Freud

In September of 2022, The New York Times *reported the story of a man, 70, who for years had been phoning 9–1–1 from his tiny apartment in midtown Manhattan to report every manner of emergency in a building 60 blocks uptown that doesn't exist. There was a murder; someone was beating up and robbing a woman in her 90s; a mentally ill woman was standing stark naked and cutting herself; a fire had started; there was a bomb. The calls prompted the dispatch of the appropriate first responders, who found nothing. The man was traced and caught, and 9–1–1 ceased sending help, but the man posed no immediate threat to himself or others and therefore could not be locked up or otherwise restrained.*

Noteworthy in the article is the way the dedicated professionals – attorneys, judges, social workers – working on the case had come to understand it. The reporter, Michael Wilson, describing one of the man's calls from June 2021 about a terror cell he imagined to be operating from the fictional address, details the call and then muses on its possible meaning:

> *"'Please send the police. 3–1–2 Riverside Drive' . . . 'I'm downstairs in the basement. I'm security. I'm watching the people in Room 340. There's people up there with a bomb.'"*

"'I'm security,'" the reporter goes on to reflect, as he reprises the promise and then gradual demise of the now shattered vestige of a human being making the calls. Then he continues:

> *"'I'm security.'"*

DOI: 10.4324/9781003394402-12

> *"In creating a place called 312 Riverside Drive, a 70-year-old recovering addict with bad legs has built a world that terrifies him day and night.*
>
> *"And yet, the invisible place that has taken so much from him has given him something as well. At 312 Riverside, [the man] is part of a community of men and women who very desperately need him.*
>
> *"Here, he is vital, and he is important. He is the help that is always on the way."*
>
> (Wilson, 2022, p. A19)

The man, in other words, might have gained from his bewildering and devastating machinations a measure of relief. That prospect could explain why he might have persisted in behavior that brought him no evident reward and indeed the despair and denunciation of those attempting to grapple with the nuisance he created.

The whole idea that the man gained something from his activity and that it might have been born of that purpose is essential Freud.

Freud left behind a systematic theory of the mind elegant in its simplicity and rich and expansive in its reach. When examined on its own terms, it defies the reductive readings often applied to it. It in fact turns out to be the opposite of such a description. To say we observe a pleasure principle is not in any way to propose that we only seek pleasure, for example. It, like other designations of Freud's, is a first principle, the start of a line of reasoning about our behavior, and not the end of it. It is to say that we can understand our behavior by looking for its payoff, as the *Times* reporter writes about the phantom caller.

Freud built his theory in ever widening circles around his core idea of avoiding harm, or what he called unpleasure; he soon deemed it nearly as fundamental to seek or reproduce pleasure, loosely speaking. He added what he called instincts to the conception, endogenous urges roughly translatable at the most basic level to sex and survival – both terms being far more broadly meant than we are accustomed to conceiving them. As stimuli we will naturally seek to discharge, they set the psychic apparatus in motion. But satisfying them is complicated, so achieving that satisfaction triggers development.

As our minds develop, we continue to want, as well as to monitor our wants for the likely consequences of pursuing them and to adjust our actions accordingly. We also become self-observers and appraisers, an internalization, Freud thinks, of our early dependency on our parents and the complicated internal dynamic that attended the dependency. He represents those different tiers of interest as id, ego, and superego.

Freud added later refinements to the pleasure principle – our core tendency to avoid harm and strive for the pleasurable or useful. He made two observations that prompted the changes. One was the recognition that pleasure is more complicated than the physiological definition he first assigned it, which coupled the accession to pleasure with the discharge of excitation. The other was his discovery that we are driven at times by a compulsion to repeat that can override the striving for pleasure. He consequently rearranged the theory with an anchor in the buildup and discharge of excitation, the life and death instincts, respectively. The striving for pleasure, or release from unpleasure, still primary psychologically, now reflected an intermixing of the life and death instincts, as did the human capacity for aggression.

It makes sense that a pleasure principle would be the first tenet of a psychology. When we ask "why" somebody did something, we are looking for the aim or the purpose the action served. Why did Max go to the jeweler? He needed a battery for his watch, which doesn't need any interpretation. Why does he continue to pursue Brenda when he doesn't love her? In that case we are looking for an answer in terms of Max's perceptions, thoughts, and needs. Why does he *always* continue to pursue relationships after he has lost his zest for them? To answer the last question, we might feel tempted to look for interpersonal patterns across Max's life or possibly to examine his first relationships as a small child.

Freud was as much clinician, scientist, and social observer as he was a theoretician. We saw the sensitive practitioner alert to every nuance in patients' behavior, bearing, and communication, and the compassionate and resourceful counselor. He was a scientist not in that he ran controlled studies in a lab, but in the meticulous and methodical way he observed and dissected behavior piece by piece and from multiple angles until he found and then solved its riddle. As a social observer, he had the courage to apply what he knew of the psyche to address the prospects for society.

We can understand from the pleasure principle as just summarized how Freud approached his neurotic patients, people exhibiting tendencies that appeared maladaptive and even nonsensical on the outside, like the refusal of a perfectly able woman – Anna O. – to drink. He wanted to know the problem the tendencies were solving for the patients. Only then would it become feasible to free the patients from the maladaptive cycle. When Freud and Breuer and their patients traced the patients' ailments to their potentially germinating contexts, patients obtained relief.

Freud asked similar questions of the content of dreams. He wanted to know which material from dreamers' ongoing thoughts gave sense to their dreams. What problem did the imagery solve, what did the dreamer gain by it? He analyzed dreams down to their tiniest detail, finding a place for each in the emerging tapestry.

Given that dreaming is a completely involuntary activity and occurs when the mind is on standby, we cannot know that dreams form for the specific purpose of expressing the sense dreamers later make of them.[1] What we do know is that dreamers' attempts to locate them in the stream of their mental lives is often revelatory and fruitful. We know that dreams, arising from a process so different from conscious waking thought, may also evoke associations to material not evident to conscious thought and thereby open new pathways of self-understanding (Freud, 1900, p. 608).

Freud used the same investigative strategy, of looking for the gain achieved from behavior, when exploring fragments of ordinary waking mental life.

When we accidentally say one word and mean another, we may have an interfering intention that agrees with the word said. When we suddenly can't recall a name we know well, some line of thought within us may occasion a fright that encompasses the forgotten name or something related to it, causing us to pull away from it. Any of those kinds of little errors may be more simply explained. However, interference of the sort Freud considers could materialize, and pursuing it even as a mere possibility can direct us to other strands of thought that merit our attention.

Similarly for other segments of our lives. Jokes, it turns out on inspection, have a particular form. What might be the pleasure in it, and why does our pleasure manifest specifically in the form of laughter? Why – again why – do we become lost in a book, unable to tear ourselves away, even when we know we must? What are we getting out of it that has us so entranced, as if in a daydream? We *are* daydreaming according to Freud and are hence mesmerized.

In addressing societal dynamics in *Civilization and Its Discontents*, Freud turns his attention to the inevitability and ubiquity of the thwarting of our attempts to become happy or at least escape misery. The obstacles come not only from the social sphere we have built and its demands, but also and perhaps more persistently from the way our minds negotiate that sphere. Yet the latter inhibitions answer a purpose – to avert a different pain or threat – with the result that we end up creatures in interminable conflict. It is a way of being we might think we would have been loath to choose, yet it is what inexorably happens and is the stuff of which our finer sensibilities are built.

By now so many of Freud's concepts and teachings pervade both the popular and professional lexicon that his innovations are easily overlooked. His way of thought and the field he created – psychoanalysis – live on in the very fiber of the discipline, regardless of how far it might imagine it has strayed from him. We would not ask how people's way of assimilating information makes them see and behave as they do or how that way of assimilating might have been conditioned by their earlier experiences had Freud not written. Although schools of psychoanalytic thought may differ with respect to which earlier experiences and which motifs are likely to signify, the idea that some do and may be elicited from their bearers and explored comes from the schools' common forebear.

Freud's contribution could also be combed further for its riches. His theory, so full of nuance and intricacy and an elegance of construction, is often misread, still. His writings – as opposed to their distillation in secondary sources – contain a shrewdness and depth of argument that rivals the best conceptual discourse. He gives us a way to explore psychological questions through reasoning and example that go to the interior and subjective. He is worth reading, not only for the foundations of the field he created and the sensitive and hopeful means he developed to relieve human suffering, but also for the way he thought.

Note

1 I discuss this quandary at length in Sugarman (2023).

References

The abbreviation *SE* refers in this book to *The Standard Edition of the Complete Psychological Works of Sigmund Freud*, J. Strachey, Trans. and General Ed. London: Hogarth, 1981.

Beigel, H.G. (1953). Sex and human beauty. *J. Aesthet. Art Crit., 12*, 1, 83–92.

Bion, W.R. (1984). *Learning from Experience*. London: Karnac. Originally published 1962.

Bowlby, J. (1969). *Attachment and Loss: Vol. 1. Attachment*. New York: Basic.

Breuer, J., and Freud, S. (1895). Studies in hysteria. In J. Strachey (Gen. Ed. and Trans.), *The Standard Edition of the Complete Psychological Works of Sigmund Freud (SE)*, Vol. II. London: Hogarth, 1981.

Domhoff, G.W. (2019). The neurocognitive theory of dreams at age 20: An assessment and a comparison with four other theories of dreaming. *Dreaming, 29*, 265-302.

Erikson, E. (1950). *Childhood and Society*. New York: Norton.

Fairbairn, W.R.D. (1994). *From Instinct to Self: Selected Papers of W.R.D. Fairbairn, Vol. 1*. (E.F. Birtles & D.E. Sharff, Eds.). Northvale, NJ: Jason Aronson.

Fechner, G.T. (1873). *Einige Ideen zur Schöpfungs- und Entwickelungsgeschichte der Organismen*. Leipzig: Druck und verlag von Breitkopf und Haertel.

Freud, S. (1891). *On Aphasia: A Critical Study* (E. Stengel, Trans.). New York: International Universities Press, 1953.

Freud, S. (1895). Project for a Scientific Psychology. *SE*, I, 295–397.

Freud, S. (1900). The Interpretation of Dreams. *SE*, IV–V.

Freud, S. (1901). The Psychopathology of Everyday Life. *SE*, VI.

Freud, S. (1905a). Three Essays on the Theory of Sexuality. *SE*, VII, 125–246.

Freud, S. (1905b). Jokes and Their Relation to the Unconscious. *SE*, VIII.

Freud, S. (1906). Psychopathic Characters on the Stage. *SE*, VII, 305–310.

Freud, S. (1908a). Creative Writers and Daydreaming. *SE*, IX, 143–153.

Freud, S. (1908b). Character and Anal Eroticism. *SE*, IX, 169–175.

Freud, S. (1909a). Five Lectures on Psychoanalysis. *SE*, XI, 3–56.

Freud, S. (1909b). Notes Upon a Case of Obsessional Neurosis. *SE*, X, 153–318.

Freud, S. (1911). Formulations Regarding the two Principles in Mental Functioning. *SE*, XII, 213–226.

Freud, S. (1914). On Narcissism: An Introduction. *SE*, XIV, 67–102.

Freud, S. (1915). Instincts and Their Vicissitudes. *SE*, XIV, 109–140.

Freud, S. (1916). On Transience. *SE*, XIV, 303–307.

Freud, S. (1917a). Mourning and Melancholia. *SE*, XIV, 237–258.

Freud, S. (1917b). Introductory Lectures on Psychoanalysis. *SE*, XVI.

Freud, S. (1918). From the History of an Infantile Neurosis. *SE*, XVII, 1–122.

Freud, S. (1919). The "Uncanny." *SE*, XVII, 217–256.

Freud, S. (1920). Beyond the Pleasure Principle. *SE*, XVIII, 3–64.

Freud, S. (1921). Group psychology and the Analysis of the Ego. *SE*, XVIII, 65–143.

Freud, S. (1923). The Ego and the Id. *SE*, XIX, 3–66.

Freud, S. (1924). The Economic Problem in Masochism. *SE*, XIX, 157–170.

Freud, S. (1925). Negation. *SE*, XIX, 233–249.

Freud, S. (1927). The Future of an Illusion. *SE*, XXI, 1–56.

Freud, S. (1930). Civilization and Its Discontents. *SE*, XXI, 57–145.

Freud, S. (1936). A Disturbance of Memory on the Acropolis: An Open Letter to Romain Rolland on the Occasion of his Seventieth Birthday. *SE*, XXII, 237–248.

Freud, S. (1939). Moses and Monotheism. *SE*, XXIII, 1–137.

Freud, S. (1940). An Outline of Psychoanalysis. *SE*, XXIII, 141–207.

Hartmann, H. (1939). *Ego psychology and the problem of adaptation* (D. Rappaport, Trans.). New York: International Universities Press.

Heymans, G. (1896). Ästhetische Untersuchungen in Anschluss an ie Lippssche Theorie des Komischen. *Z. Psychol. Physiol. Sinnesart.*, *11*, 31, 333.

Hobson, J. A. ((1988). *The dreaming brain: How the brain creates both the sense and the nonsense of dreams.* New York: Basic Books.

Hume, D. (1739). *A Treatise of Human Nature* (L.A. Selby-Bigge, P.H. Nidditch, Eds.). Oxford: Oxford/Clarendon, 1978 (2nd ed.).

Jacobson, E. (1964). *The Self and the Object World.* New York: International Universities Press.

Klein, M. (1957). *Envy and Gratitude and Other Works: 1946–1963.* New York: Delacourt, 1975.

Kohut, H. (1984). *How Does Analysis Cure?* New York: International Universities Press.

Lear, J. (2000). *Happiness, Death, and the Remainder of Life.* Cambridge, MA: Harvard University Press.

Loewald, H. (1988). *Sublimation.* New Haven: Yale University Press.

Low, B. (1920). *Psychoanalysis: A Brief Account of the Freudian Theory*. New York: Harcourt-Brace.

Mahler, M. (1968). *On Human Symbiosis and the Vicissitudes of Individuation. Vol. 1. Infantile Psychosis*. New York: International Universities Press.

Mitchell, S.A., and Black, M.J. (1995). *Freud and Beyond: A history of Psychoanalytic Thought*. New York: Basic Books.

Nietzsche, F. (1887), *On the Genealogy of Morality*, 3rd ed. (K. Ansell-Pearson, Ed., C. Diethe, Trans.). Cambridge: Cambridge University Press, 2017.

Solms, M., and Turnbull, O. (2007). To sleep, perchance to REM? The rediscovered role of emotion and meaning in dreams. In S. Della Sala (Ed.)), *Tall tales about the mind and brain*. Oxford: Oxford University Press, 472-500.

Spitz, R.A. (1965) (in collaboration with W.G. Cobliner). *The First Year of Life: A Psychoanalytic Study of Normal and Deviant Development of Object Relations*. New York: International Universities Press.

Stern, D.B. (1985). *The Interpersonal World of the Infant: A View from Psychoanalysis and Developmental Psychology*. New York: Basic Books.

Sugarman, S. (2010). *Freud on the Psychology of Ordinary Mental Life*. New York: Rowan and Littlefield.

Sugarman, S. (2016). *What Freud Really Meant: A Chronological Reconstruction of His Theory of the Mind*. Cambridge: Cambridge University Press.

Sugarman, S. (2023). *Freud's Interpretation of Dreams: A Reappraisal*. Cambridge: Cambridge University Press.

Wilson, M. (2022). Bomb scare, murder, fights: Thousands of 911 calls at one site. *The New York Times*, Vol. CLXXI, No. 59, 547, September 15, 2022, A1, A19.

Index

abreaction 49, 54
aggression
    alloy of life and death instincts,
        as 35, 36–37
    inborn, as 37
    instinct theory, in 35–38
    problem in civilization, as 89, 92
    universal love doctrine and
        93–95
anal eroticism 91
anxiety dreams *see* nightmares
art 90
autoeroticism 21

beauty 23, 90

case histories
    Anna O. 8–10, 61
    Elisabeth von R. 43–55
    Rat Man 56
    Wolf Man 70
character traits 91
civilization; *see also* aggression;
    guilt; happiness, pursuit of;
    universal love
    curtailing of instinct by 91–91,
        103
    love and necessity, founded in
        92–93
comic, the *see* jokes
compulsion to repeat 34, 35, 103
consciousness
    nature of 59
constancy principle 36

death instinct 35, 36, 94
    defined 34–35
dreams
    censorship in 65, 68
    compromise formations in 65
    convenience, of 60
    distortion in 65, 68, 68
    distressing 66–69
    early memories, evocative
        of 58
    indifferent 62–65
    jokes, parallels between 57
    method of interpreting 57, 103
    neurotic symptoms, compared
        57
    pleasure principle, and 57, 69
    royal road to unconscious, as
        70
    traumatic neurosis, in 34
    wish-fulfillments, as 60,
        64–70
dreams, specific
    income-tax return, false 67
    Irma's injection 59–60
    medical student and hospital
        61
    supper party 66
    uncle with the yellow beard
        62–66

ego instincts 25
    basal, as 20–21
    reality principle, and 25
Eros 36; *see also* life instincts

forgetting of names 75; *see also*
    parapraxes

gain from illness 104; *see also*
    pleasure principle
guilt 30
    aggression, as barrier against
        95–96, 97–99
    aggression, inward directed,
        as 97
    development of 98–99, 100–101
    problem in civilization, as 104

hallucination
    dreams, in 12
    early mental state, as 10–11
happiness, pursuit of 10–11, 21, 37,
    90–91
health, psychological *see*
    psychological health
humor *see* jokes
hypnosis 7, 8, 45, 47, 82
hysteria; *see also* case histories:
    Anna O.; Elisabeth von R.
    defined 10
    diagnosis of 44

id, ego, superego 96, 97, 103
    defined 34–36
    development of 35
identification 29
in statu nascendi 82
incentive bonus (of text), 85
instinct
    compulsion to repeat, and 35
instincts
    basal (sexual and ego), 20, 33
    civilization curtailment of 95–97
    defined 20–21
    developmental motor, as 14,
        24, 103
    pleasure principle, and 10
introjection 30

jokes 76, 77–78, 105
    childhood mentation, reversion
        to, in 80
    condensation in 77, 83
    dreams, parallels between 98

laughter at 81, 105
pleasure, sources of, in 81–84
    recognition of the familiar as
        pleasure source in 86–7
    reduction as means of analyzing
        73, 75
    savings of psychical energy in
        48, 53, 65, 79–81
    techniques of 81–83
    tendentious vs. innocent 79–81
    unconscious, role of in 82–83
jokes, specific
    home-roulard 80
    pastry shop 78
    sujet (Louis XV), 78
    tête-à-bête 77–78, 79–80, 80
    torch of truth 80
    traduttore-traditore 79

laughter *see* jokes: laughter at
life instincts 36, 37, 91
    defined 34
lost in story, getting 84, 85–87, 105
    children's play and 96–97
    daydreaming, and 85–86, 105
    wish-fulfillment, in 97, 98

masochism 39
morality 29–30, 95–96
    nature of 29–30
mourning 87

narcissism 21, 95
needs *see* instincts
negative therapeutic reaction 33
neurosis; *see also* case histories;
    hysteria; obsessive-compulsive
    disorder
    and pleasure principle 9–10
    repression, and 8
    withdrawal from reality in 15
nightmares 33, 67–68
Nirvana principle 36

obsessive-compulsive disorder 7,
    56, 98
Oedipal conflict 29–30
omnipotence, assertion of 95; *see
    also* narcissism

paradoxical surprise at the real 87
parapraxes 73, 74–75, 84–85
    neurotic symptoms, compared
        with 75–76
pleasure
    alloy of life and death instincts,
        as 37–47, 94
    lowering of excitation, as 11
    redefined 34
pleasure principle 37, 38, 102–103,
    105–106
    basic, as 15–16
    cognitive capability, and 13–14
    defined 10
    emotional connections, and
        21–23
    exception to 33–34
    instincts, and 22
    pursuit of happiness, and 90
    reality principle, and 11–14
    redefined 34
    reflex, and 10–12, 15
psychoanalysis
    discipline, as 9, 80, 52, 106–7
    modern 11, 14–15, 70–71,
        85–86
psychoanalytic therapy 22, 69,
    106–107; *see also* talking
    therapy
psychological health 38, 55
psychosis 15

reaction formation 93
reality principle 25
    and instincts 19
    development of 11–13, 29
religion 30, 90

repetition compulsion *see*
    compulsion to repeat
repression 8
resistance 8, 51

sadism 94
sexual instincts 21, 37; *see also*
    anal eroticism; autoeroticism;
    instincts; narcissism; Oedipal
    conflict
    basal, as 22–23
    reality principle, and 25
sexuality *see* sexual instincts
slips of the tongue 73; *see also*
    parapraxes
sublimation 23, 91
superego
    definition expanded 20
    development of 28–30
    higher and lower, as 29
    severity of 125–126

talking therapy 45; *see also*
    psychoanalysis: rules of
    treatment
traumatic neurosis 34

uncanny, experience of the 73, 87
unconscious
    designation of 8, 12, 25, 102
universal love, doctrine of 93–94, 95

wish; *see also* wish-fulfillment
    first embodiment of 12
wish-fulfillment
    dreams, in 57, 58–70
    getting lost in story, in 84, 87

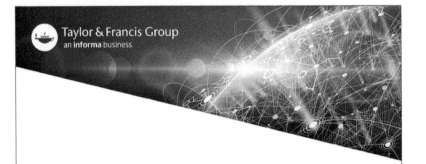

For Product Safety Concerns and Information please contact our EU
representative GPSR@taylorandfrancis.com
Taylor & Francis Verlag GmbH, Kaufingerstraße 24, 80331 München, Germany

www.ingramcontent.com/pod-product-compliance
Ingram Content Group UK Ltd.
Pitfield, Milton Keynes, MK11 3LW, UK
UKHW021041100625
459499UK00014B/154

* 9 7 8 1 0 3 2 4 9 5 4 7 7 *